BELIEVING
IN THE DARK

ROSEMARY SHERROD

MILK & HONEY
BOOKS

Cover Design: Rosemary Sherrod
Chapter Image: Deposit Photos/Lena Tru

This book is available through: www.milkandhoneybooks.com and other online retailers

Print ISBN 13: 978-1-953000-21-7
Ebook ISBN 13: 978-1-953000-22-4

For Worldwide Distribution

DEDICATION

This book is dedicated to God the Most High, my El Roi (because He has seen me in all of my troubles and afflictions). I dedicate this book to my oldest son, Qe'Vonte Tanner, because you are my sonshine and the reason it is written, and to all of my beautiful children: Xzavier, my dear son, who is compassionate and the protector of the family; Kayla, my daughter, who is brave, and exudes an inner strength beyond her years, and Caliyah, my bonus daughter, who is brilliant, kind hearted, and strong.

Table of Contents

FOREWORD

*"And we are writing these things
so that our joy may be complete."*
—1 John 1:4 (ESV)

Coping with the loss of a child may be one of the hardest challenges that a parent has to face. Even though loss is a natural part of life, it leads to prolonged periods of sadness or depression. The death of Qe'Vonte, regardless of the cause or his age, was painful and overwhelming for his mother, family and friends. It is a reality that death is a devastating ordeal because you have to accept the fact that your loved one has moved beyond the years of promise, hopes, and dreams you knew he would accomplish. The complexity and depth of grief are beyond what words can express.

Here is a mother with strong bonds of love and affection that were built over twenty-three years in a relationship with her son. Believing firmly that she is responsible for her child's health and safety; she nurtured the sense of hope that there was purpose and meaning to everything she and her son would have to face during his sickness of Neuroblastoma. Keeping their minds on the goodness and promises of the Lord, they found assurance and a compassionate place in the Father's timing that He is a refuge for the oppressed, a stronghold in times of trouble" (Psalm 9:9).

When God created humanity, He created it with a good plan for us to live out. Qe'Vonte was a blessing! He changed many lives by his confessions of endurance. During his times of severe pain and sickness, he showed forth a message of love and strength, a new way to find joy in suffering, and a new way to look at the difficulty of sickness in a positive way. Nothing can be more devastating than the death and loss of a child who knew how to bring joy, peace and happiness to any one he was around. The overwhelming suffering and intense emotions that flooded these precious lives for days, weeks, months, and years brought with them a range of different and ongoing challenges. Yet, believing the awesome Hand of God, they cried out with an amazing faith, "We won't stop believing God!"

Darkness is almost a monster waiting to swallow you whole. But, God always comforts us when we are brokenhearted, sad, depressed, and almost ready to give up. He has promised to bring us out of darkness into a marvelous light, being able to come directly into His presence without fear. In Lamentations 3, we are reminded that God's mercies are new every day. Even when things look bleak, God has promised joy will come in the morning.

Getting comforted by others is not wrong, and God will place kind believers in our path to weep with us and help us, but we always need to turn to God as our ultimate comforter.

This is what Rosemary did. Knowing others would experience all kinds of difficult and unexpected emotions, from shock or anger to unbelief- Rosemary wanted to ease another person's pain, by sharing Qe'Vonte's battle with a cancer that was developing from immature nerve cells found in several parts of his body—

Neuroblastoma. She found comfort in the fact that Jesus made the necessary preparations to receive her son when his life on Earth would come to an end. Standing on "HOPE" ...with a deep sense of peace, a righteous hope that is solid, firm and eternal ... Rosemary knew the "Hope of Glory" was strong enough to give the assurance that death is not the final word.

Surviving the death and loss of Qe'Vonte ... with a constant hunger and dedication to the Word of God for strength and purpose, this amazing book *Believing in The Dark* was birthed.

In spite of sickness, pain, frustrations and woes ... this mother found wonderful things in the darkness through her son's overshadowing faith. According to Deuteronomy 5: 22, God is the One who dwells in thick darkness.

> *Even the darkness is not dark to Him. And the night is as bright as the day. Darkness and light are alike to Him.*
> *—Psalm 139:12*

Walking by faith and not by sight, this mother knew her beautiful son heard the Voice of God at the end of the tunnel saying, "Well done, you good and faithful servant. Enter into the joy of your Lord."

God doesn't mind us asking for courage to go through the darkness. HE will prepare us to obey no matter how we feel. The Word of God assures us that Jesus cares for us, and we can go through whatever life has to offer and make the most of it! Be encouraged ... ultimately ... you will come out of the darkness into a greater sense of light than you had when you went in.

Believing in the Dark is such a wonderful written testimony for others to know ... you too can be a witness to the anointing that enables you to endure any obstacle as you hold on to God's unchanging hand. Darkness may come, but with God all things can become possible to those who believe. It is a must that we remember—what God has prepared for us is so much greater than anything we are going to experience in this life. The hope that we have in Christ Jesus will keep us holding on and pressing forward toward our eternal reward.

—Pastor Evangelist Emma White
Redeeming Love Outreach Ministries

INTRODUCTION

"When I sit in darkness,
The Lord will be a light to me."
— Micah 7:8 (NKJV)

One evening, after getting settled in from a long day, I was anticipating sitting on my front porch to relax and enjoy some quiet time. I actually planned to organize some concepts for this book as I enjoyed a moment of peace. As I approached the door, my oldest son, Qe'Vonte asked me what I had planned for dinner. I longed for some fresh air and time away from the kids to consider what I would write next. I was racing to beat the night sky from settling in. Now if you knew my son, you would know that this was code for, "Ma, I'm hungry." So I responded quickly with an impromptu menu, to reassure him that I was on top of it.

At that time he was recovering from neurosurgery and was still regaining strength. I didn't want him even attempting to cook (as it was one of his favorite things to do for himself). If he thought for one second that I had other plans, he would have been out of the bed determined to prepare his own food. I was becoming irritated because I wanted to have everything finished before sunset. I wasn't bothered by Qe, but mainly that I had yet again allowed time to slip away from me. I could see dusk fading into dark by the minute.

Once dinner was finished, I ran out to the porch and plopped in my chair to relax and soak in the few minutes of daylight I had left. I immediately felt the Holy Spirit posing the question, "Why were you in such a rush?" The first answer that came to mind was "I don't want to sit in the dark." In my relationship with the Father, I've come to realize the Holy Spirit's questions are to offer me an enlightening lesson. I looked deeper into my answer. What was it about the dark that bothered me so much?

As I looked within for answers, this is what came to me…I didn't want to sit in the dark because of what might be lurking there. I didn't want bugs to sneak up on me (I was terrified of strange bugs). They tend to come out in droves in the mid-summer South. I also didn't live in the best part of town, so the thought of encountering an unwanted guest was an unwelcome possibility. I was often stopped and asked if I had spare change. There were also a couple of shootings that had taken place on my block.

Not to mention, my neighbor fed tons of cats that often tried to take residence on my porch. Over the years, I'd become not too fond of cats. It was like these cats knew I didn't like them, and the more I disliked them the more they invaded my space. They would be under my car, on my roof, and in the bushes. It may sound strange, but the point is that I felt more vulnerable in the dark to the things that made me feel uncomfortable. Things that I didn't like by day seemed to be more threatening to me by night. Sitting in the dark made me more acutely aware of this in the most uncomfortable way.

The Holy Spirit was showing me something valuable. God was revealing a parallel to why believing in the dark is so uncomfortable as well. Believing in an environment in which our physical senses are limited is equivalent to what it means to walk by faith and not by sight. Sight isn't helpful when you're believing God for a miracle. It wouldn't be called a miracle if it were easy to see or obtain.

Now faith is the substance of things hoped for, the evidence of things not seen. Hebrews 11:1 (NKJV)

What is believing in the dark? It is believing in the best outcome when you don't know what tomorrow holds. Believing when the situation you are facing is worsening day by day. Believing when the pain increases. Believing when you're not sure if you have the strength to continue to believe. Believing when the vast majority doesn't believe or has stopped believing. Believing when you wonder if you're crazy for still believing. Believing when it goes against the grain of everything that makes sense — this is believing in the dark. Believing when you can't see the end of your story.

When I speak of believing in the dark, I am choosing to meditate on the only truth that has been proven, which is God's infallible Word. When we learn to pay closer attention to Scripture, rather than what's screaming at us in the dark, it provides direction to us in the darkest situations. Though I knew God, walked with Him, and considered myself to have strong faith—I was challenged greatly. Believing in the dark is a process of fine-tuning your faith's focus.

The season where I found myself believing for my son's life was the darkest season I had ever experienced in my life. What I saw with my eyes and heard from the doctors with my ears put my faith to the test like never before. At one point, I felt like I was relearning what it meant to have faith in God. I remember stealing away to meditate on God's Word concerning healing. Immediately following, I felt strengthened to face the battle again. But not long after, another doctor's report would knock the wind out of me. I often thought, "This is it. You might as well stop believing." God used a dark situation to stretch me beyond belief.

The emotional turmoil I experienced from watching my son suffer with cancer caused me to shed countless tears. I would often evaluate the reason for my tears as if I was probing my heart for whether any unbelief existed. Was I crying because I didn't believe or trust God? No, my tears were just a result of my pain. I knew God was looking at my faith throughout this journey, and I wanted Him to always find me believing Him for the miraculous. When I poured out my heart with tears, it was because I absolutely hated seeing my son in pain while suffering from this disease, not because I was ever lacking in faith.

Qe'Vonte was truly one of the brightest human beings I have ever encountered. In the season I reference as our darkest, almost every doctor's report felt like a boulder crashing into a building to tear it down. There were times when we received highlights such as "surgery went well; it hasn't spread" or "everything is stable." Those were the reports that gave us the strength to keep fighting and believing. They were the silver linings painted behind some pretty dark clouds. I would latch on to those moments like a pit bull and press on, believing that God would bring my son through this with a victorious end.

My faith walk felt much like that moment on my front porch

when I realized how uncomfortable it was to sit in darkness. When your vision is impaired, it's as if all other senses become heightened. When you're in your dark season, allow your spiritual senses to be heightened through prayer and faith. When walking through your dark seasons, it is imperative that you have something concrete to illuminate your path. For me, that was the Word of God.

Your word is a lamp to my feet and a light to my path.
Psalm 119:105 (NIV)

Though a time of darkness has its many discomforts, I also learned that it has its many blessings. There were many hidden gems that would come alive and be revealed in the darkness. The average person tends to seek out and crave seasons of ease and happiness. But rarely do you hear of anyone asking for hard times or suffering. I reflected on what my natural fears were as I sat on my porch that night. But more importantly, I pinpointed the fears that could hinder my faith's biggest fight yet. I decided I would not be controlled by fear, but by faith.

Beauty blooms in the nighttime as well as in the dark times we will face in life. If I fixated only on my fears, I wouldn't have seen some of the beautiful things that surfaced. I challenged my fears and faced them in faith. I stayed honest about where I was in my prayers to God, and I believe this is what helped me see beauty in my darkness.

Did you know there are flowers that only bloom at night? Yes, and they all have an exquisite beauty. Most of them have a very unique sweet-smelling fragrance as well. Sometimes we can think nothing good can come out of our dark seasons, but if we shift our focus and remove our fears from our focal point, God will begin to reveal to us the beauty and fragrance blooming in our darkness.

PROTECTING WHAT
YOU BELIEVE

E arly on in my walk with Christ, I learned the power of words. From the first day Qe'Vonte was diagnosed with cancer, I began to utilize this power by speaking life because I understood that my words were one of my greatest weapons. Proverbs 18:21 says that death and life are in the power of the tongue, and those who love it will eat its fruit. The goal was for Qe to eat the fruit of God's healing power.

Qe'Vonte was eight years old when he was diagnosed with neuroblastoma. This is a rare disease that most commonly affects young children. During the first few years of this journey, I wasn't fully aware of neuroblastoma's reputation. I had such a focus on Qe'Vonte's healing process that I didn't realize how blessed his journey was until years later. Every year, approximately 800 children ages 0 to 14 are diagnosed with neuroblastoma in the United States. It accounts for 6% of all childhood cancers.

Neuroblastoma's survival rate is 81%, which is dependent on many factors. It is the third most common type of cancer in children.[1]

From the moment he was diagnosed, my instincts to protect him were heightened in every possible way. Of course, as a mother, I was already protective of all three of my children. But when you realize something is threatening their safety, the mama bear in you rises to do battle on their behalf. In 2004, late one night, Qe woke me up several times to tell me that he had pains in his back. I initially thought he had slept in a wrong position that resulted in a cramp of some sort. After I had told him to go back to bed several times, he began to cry from the pain. This was out of character for him, and I realized that something must be majorly wrong. I took him to the local hospital emergency room.

My best friend Boniechia lived close by, and she came with me. After performing some scans, the doctor informed me that there was a tumor the size of a small baseball in his right lung and that I needed to follow up with Birmingham Children's Hospital in Birmingham, Alabama. As the doctor explained the details, I was trying to process the news and the meaning of the medical terminology. I remember having to ask what benign meant. (For those of you who are as ill-informed as I was, benign means non-cancerous.) It was a relief to hear that it wasn't cancerous.

I had never known anyone with cancer before, so I was completely clueless about the subject matter. When the doctor left the room, Boniechia and I stood on each side of his bed and prayed over his little body. We had just heard a sermon about the protection of God over our lives and how we are to seek shelter "under His wings." As an act of faith, we prayed over Qe and began to move our arms back and forth (in flying motion) to represent God's wings of protection over his life.

I will abide in Your tabernacle forever;
I will trust in the shelter of Your wings. Selah
—Psalm 61:4 (NKJV)

I immediately started focusing on having faith to see my son through this. After the emergency room visit, I scheduled an initial visit to Birmingham Children's Hospital. After his first consultation, they scheduled surgery to remove the baseball-sized mass in his lung. After its removal, they said they did find some malignant (cancerous) cells and believed that they had removed it all but were not entirely sure. The plan was to evaluate and follow up to watch his progress. After his first surgery, as they were rolling him back into the room, I remember how vulnerable he looked. He hadn't woken up yet from the anesthesia and seeing him like that was overwhelming. He had never been sick before, besides having a common cold. To go from that to major surgery was hard to witness. He looked so frail as he lay there with a dried-up tear on his cheek. I became so emotional that I rushed outside in tears. I felt like my heart had been pierced. As I sat outside the hospital, I looked up at the night sky and cried out for my little boy.

From that moment on, I did everything in my power to protect his space as I believed God for healing to come to fruition. My guard was against doubt and negativity because I knew how powerful words were in this tender process of believing. I could especially feel the mama bear rising within me if someone began to speak doubt or negativity over the situation.

Mama bears have gained quite a reputation for being aggressively protective over their cubs. So much so that we've adopted the phrase "mama bear" when associating a mother's intense desire to fight for her child. One thing that's rarely talked about is why her fight is so aggressive. Why has she developed such a reputation? Because her cubs' lives are always threatened by adult male bears (boars.) Boars kill cubs so that they can mate with the female again, and I know the thought of this is horrible. I can only imagine how the mama bear's natural instincts sharpened over time due to this threat. I could relate to the mother bear's plight as I reflected on her struggle to keep her cubs alive.

Years passed in which Qe was in and out of remission. Even during the time he was in remission, the continuous checkups and doctor appointments reminded me that there was an enemy to keep at bay. Cancer was like the evil boar in the backdrop of our lives, and I was determined to keep it away. When there's a constant threat, you naturally become overprotective. But you also become more fearless.

I once read a story of a mama bear that was attacked while fishing in the river with her cub. While the mom fought the boar, the cub climbed a nearby tree. After the ferocious fight, the mom joined her cub. They hung out in the tree for a few hours. Just when she thought the coast was clear, she returned to the river only to find that several boars were now in the area. She didn't shrink back in fear but continued fishing for her cub in confidence. It's my sincere prayer that my fight will be as confident and fearless in the midst of adversity.

All things become possible for those who believe. I believed that I would see Qe experience milestones throughout his adolescence, and I was determined that he would obtain every tangible goal possible. Each time he achieved a new feat, it fortified my faith and reinforced that we would keep fighting for the future and the hope that God has promised even amid "boars."

There was one particular recurrence Qe had as a child that uniquely stood out to me. This was approximately the third time the cancer had returned. After another surgery, I watched him lying in bed, and he looked so frail. I thought this was a good time for me to find the chapel to pray while he was peacefully sleeping. As I began to pray, I felt myself unraveling as I poured out my emotions and cried out to God for my son, not caring who may have walked in or heard me. I poured out my soul before the LORD as I cried and reminded God of His word. I felt this deep reverence for God and His ability to save my son's life. I wiped my tears and went back up to his room to lie by his side. I was thankful he was still asleep, because I was exhausted.

I fell asleep and tried my best to sleep lightly enough to hear if the nurses or doctors came into the room. My exhaustion caused me to fall into a deep sleep. I was later awakened by a man that came and sat in front of me. Qe was still asleep. The man introduced himself as the hospital chaplain. He held out about five stones with words on them, and he told me to pick one that best described how I felt. As I carefully examined each stone, the words labeled on them were love, peace, hope, and grateful. I chose the stone labeled grateful.

The man made a little humph sound, and he smiled and left the room. That's it. He just smiled and left the room. His visit felt mysterious. I held that stone in my hand tightly and fell back to sleep, feeling an assurance in my heart that God was going to answer the prayer I prayed in the chapel that day. It was a process, but Qe did move forward in his healing from that day on. I often thought of the man having me choose the word that best described how I felt. I was even more glad that gratitude is what was in my heart. My perspective could have been quite different. I could have complained and been disgruntled that we were back in the hospital fighting cancer. I believe the word grateful was the most powerful, considering the trial we faced.

A few years later, I spoke at a church where I shared this particular story. After the service, a lady came to me and began to share the story of her child's battle with a terminal illness. She began to cry as she spoke. I held the stone in my hand that day as I shared my own story before the crowd. I took the stone and gave it to her. I cherished that stone because it was special to me for so many reasons. But I thought if I could pass on the same spirit of gratefulness, peace, and encouragement to another parent, this was the moment to do so. Her tears seemed to have transformed from tears of pain to tears of hope and joy.

After Qe'Vonte's second and third recurrence, the tumor's slow progression gave us peace. But cancer having recurred more than twice was a bit alarming to doctors due to neuroblastoma's aggressive reputation. Qe's doctor stated several times how rare it was that the cancer had never spread from its initial location in his right lung. In many cases, a child would not usually survive after a second bout. Gratefulness protected our journey toward healing for many unforeseen roads ahead.

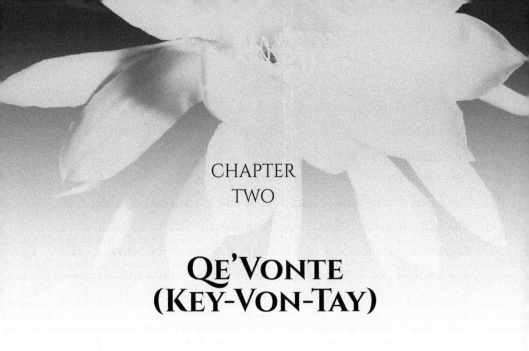

CHAPTER
TWO

QE'VONTE
(KEY-VON-TAY)

I became a mother at the age of 14, and I didn't want my first born's life to reflect the hardships I encountered. As I fought hard to overcome the common stereotypes and statistics about teen moms (ones I had both witnessed and read about), I became determined to teach my children to build a relationship with God, walk in honor, and have self-respect. I wanted them to understand that they could live lives of unlimited possibility. I tried to instill in them the idea that they could have anything in life and be who they desired to be if they sought God first, set goals, worked hard, and stayed focused. Because Qe'Vonte was my oldest, he probably received the most "life lesson" lectures from me out of all his siblings. I saw these lessons as my greatest weapon to overcome poverty.

Qe'Vonte Izaiah Tanner was a bubbly kid with a broad smile. He was known by many as "Q" or "Qe (Key)." He was the type of student that rarely needed to study and maintained an A/B average until his senior year of high school. I often warned him that his lack of studying would catch up with him someday, and in college, it finally did.

In his senior year of high school, his inner teen rebel began to challenge me. His life had been so monochromatic, I should have known he would add a pop of color to the journey someday. His grades dropped and he began to get into trouble with friends. Whenever he seemed to be losing focus, I would remind him of his goals and what it would take to accomplish them.

He expressed early on that he wanted to be a pediatric anesthesiologist. One day I asked him, "Why anesthesiology son?" He paused and said, "When I was little, I would get super nervous right before surgery. . . the anesthesiologist would always bring me comfort. I wanna be a comfort to kids in the same situation, that's why." He nodded his head yes with a reassuring smile after he finished. I wasn't sure if he had just connected those dots or had been pondering that for years, but I was impressed.

After he graduated from high school, he wavered back and forth between career options and finally decided to focus on pediatric oncology. He had a true passion for children. I was so excited at the idea of him selecting a career path that would touch children while allowing him to share his bright smile and bubbly personality. I believed that he would be such a ray of hope for children suffering battles similar to ones he had experienced in his childhood cancer journey.

As Qe went through chemo in his elementary years, children teased him because he was bald. I found out years later that his brother Xzavier would defend him by fighting anyone that dared talked about Qe. Of course the boys never told me about any of this at the time it actually happened. Xzavier shared with me how one time Qe was sitting on the curb crying one day after school. When Xzavier found out who was teasing his big brother, he not only found them, he fought them. I don't promote fighting, but I can say that I was happy to know that Xzavier had his brother's back. I'm sure this contributed to their unique bond.

One afternoon I noticed Qe wasn't himself and I said, "Son, what's wrong?" He got real quiet and said, "The girls at school don't like me. I mean, they like me . . . but not, 'boyfriend-type' like me." His little feelings were so hurt and his ego was bruised. Like any loving mama, I pointed out how handsome he was. Because I was his mom, it was never hard to console him with endless compliments. Experiences like that gave birth to one of my many nicknames for him: "Mama's beautiful boy." I never called him that publicly, but it was my private way of affirming him from an early age.

In middle school, Qe joined the Chapman Middle School's basketball team. I was excited about going to see him at basketball games to watch him in action. Those times were so cherished because we weren't going on yet another doctor's appointment for chemotherapy or radiation. Often during his games, his eyes would cut over at me to see if I was watching him play. I would smile as big as I could with a thumbs up, so he would know that I was intently watching him. Coach Blanding had this to say about Qe:

I remember the first day I met Qe'Vonte. It was during basketball turnouts his 8th-grade year. My staff and I had just gotten to Chapman Middle School a few seasons earlier and we were in the process of turning the programs around. So we were monitoring players very closely on and off the court. Qe, as he wanted to be called, had never played organized ball before, but he had a tremendous toughness about him. Any kid who could get through all of our condition workouts and has never played was tough physically and mentally.

We would keep thirteen players that season and in the seasons before and after Qe, I would only keep twelve. But there was something about Qe that I couldn't shake. He was not very skilled, but he had an energy and desire that was unmatched. Because his skill level was not where the other guys were but his desire was off the charts, I met with him and told him that I don't normally keep more than twelve players, and I definitely don't keep 8th graders who tried out for the first time and they weren't polished because we would only have one season to work with them. I told him that I wanted him to be a part of the team, but I was not sure how much he would actually have if he would play at all. The look in his eyes when we finished that conversation was like the brightest sunrise I had ever seen. He was super excited and told me that he wouldn't let me down and I wouldn't regret picking him.

He was the consummate teammate. He came bouncing down the hall every day ready to practice with that same glow in his eyes and pep in his step. When he moved on to high school he would often text me and thank me again and to check on me and the team. What an amazing kid who was so selfless and caring. If you ever saw him smile it would light up your life and you would never forget it.

Being able to see Qe enjoy being a kid made my heart smile. During his middle school years, we encountered a pleasant surprise. Qe'Vonte had an amazing ear for music, and he taught himself piano. He was blessed to later have two mentors that helped him with his music journey. Mr. Brian Lyles (music teacher at Chapman Middle School) and Jemeana Roberson (our church's music director/teen bible study teacher at the time). They both invested invaluable time tutoring Qe and training him in his talent. Another dear friend, Corrie Thorne, gave him free piano lessons that I was tremendously grateful for. I hoped for his gift in music to propel him toward his purpose. Later, I even put him in piano lessons to help cultivate his gift. Paying for piano lessons is no small job for a single mom struggling to make ends meet. But my prayer was that someday he would play for church, or perhaps piano might help secure scholarships for college.

Qe attended Lee High School in 2010. Lee is a magnet school for students that are gifted in the area of the arts. It was there at Lee High that he continued to cultivate his love for music by joining the band. He connected quickly to the music teacher, Mr. Knots. According to stories Qe shared with me, it appeared that Mr. Knots challenged him and also had to put Qe's ego in check a few times. I knew Qe could get a little full of himself, and get puffed up on occasion. I appreciated the discipline he'd receive from the men in his life like his dad and the many mentors God placed in his path.

His high school years were as normal as his peers except for the periodic doctor appointments to monitor his remission. One morning while dropping him off at school I heard a girl say in a flirtatious tone, "Hey Q," with a small wave. From that day forward, I concluded that girls were definitely no longer teasing him. He had a slim athletic build and long dreadlocks. He chose to grow his hair into locs in his early teens. Initially, I wanted him to keep a clean haircut. But after his continuous urging to grow his hair, I asked him, "Son, why locs?" He shared how he was never able to grow it out because of the countless chemotherapy treatments and that he loved the rasta style. He said he wanted to grow his hair out as long as possible.

I quickly grew to love his hair journey because of his reason. In addition, he was pretty handsome with the new look. Now he was my beautiful boy with long hair. His everyday decisions almost felt deliberate, commonly tied toward overcoming cancer, even down to details like his hair.

When Qe graduated from high school in June 2014, he immediately went on to start college during the summer semester. I encouraged him to not waste any time so that he could get schooling completed sooner than later—especially with his intense ambition to succeed in the tough and competitive field of medicine. Most importantly to me and unbeknownst to him, I noticed him starting to gravitate toward unhealthy environments that I knew could be detrimental to his future. I felt it was best for him to go away for a while. My prayer was that college would keep him focused on his dreams. He graduated on a Friday, and we headed to the University of South Alabama in Mobile on the following Tuesday.

I was so excited for him to start this new journey! He was now my college boy. I was extremely proud that Qe was setting such a great example for his siblings. I didn't want to see anything get in the way of his dream. This was a big deal for both of us for different reasons. He was excited about exercising his ambition to escape poverty, and I wanted to see him obtain the best life had to offer. I prayed that God would cover him. My greatest hope was that he would have a better life than the one I'd had. Throughout my journey as a single mother, I attempted to pick up the pieces of my life in order to achieve my own dreams. While he was in high school, I obtained my GED. I soon enrolled in a local community college, becoming a college student myself. I was hopeful and encouraged that he was achieving these milestones before I did.

I never really thought about the commonalities I shared with Qe in life until after his death. When he was conceived, I was a freshman at a magnet school for the arts in Chicago. I loved to draw, and I loved to learn. I missed 52 days of school that year due to morning sickness, which saddened me greatly. Art motivated me and helped me dream that I could get out of poverty. The possibility that I could someday turn my passion into profit gave me hope. I carried a sense of responsibility to take care of my mom and brother. I don't think any child should have to carry the weight of feeling like they have to take care of their family. But I can understand firsthand why so many do. As I lay in bed feeling like I was physically dying from morning sickness, emotionally I was mourning the death of my dreams. We both experienced trials in our youth that fueled our fire of ambition to succeed.

I went from being an innocent, inexperienced tomboy who had barely experienced her first kiss to giving birth. I was petrified. It was the next hardest thing I had to process after my father's death. Instead of being showered with gifts, I was showered with shame. The Christians in my life condemned me, the adults in my life judged me, and my peers labeled me. To say that I was lonely is an understatement. I felt unloved, unholy, and uncared for. My mom was definitely there for me but unable to truly identify with my pain or provide the comfort and direction I needed at the time. Deep within my heart, I knew I was a good person. But the people in my path didn't look at my heart; they looked at my pregnancy. To them, I was just as bad as the choices I had made. By the time I had my second child, I had become everything they accused me of being.

I barely had the gas to get Qe to the college campus, but as always, God provided right in the nick of time. My determination as a mother often manifests itself as mountain-moving faith. Lord knows I would have gotten in that car and driven six hours to Mobile, on fumes, by faith, no matter what! I was determined to get my son to the next stage of his life. I have literally done such things and money would just be deposited into my account or someone would randomly put money on my door. God has always provided for me and my children in supernatural ways, especially when times were tough.

Boniechia, affectionately referred to by Qe as "Auntie", rode with me, Qe, and "Lil Sis" Kayla to Mobile to see Qe off for school. We laughed, listened to music, and talked the entire ride. After we arrived and helped Qe unload, it was time to say our goodbyes. Qe hugged me several times and told me that he loved me. I kept asking if he needed anything else before we left. I wanted to make sure he was stocked up on snacks. My stalling was my way of savoring that milestone moment before we left. He said, "Ma, I'm straight. I promise, I'm good," with the biggest smile, reassuring me yet pushing me out the door. As I headed back to my car, tears began to fall as I felt myself loosening my grip on him. He was now six hours away, and I had to allow him room to grow into a young man. I had to trust God with this milestone called college life.

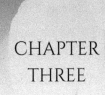

THE BOAR WAS BACK

Qe spent a few semesters at the University of South Alabama and then decided to take a break. I guess I wasn't surprised since he went straight to college just a few days after high school graduation. He lived in Mobile for a couple of years. I gave him space to find his path as an individual and as a man during this time. I wanted my sons to be productive men that would know how to carry their own weight and the weight of their families. I knew how important it was to give my sons space to figure out life on their own. I never wanted to overindulge them or cripple their development of becoming strong men.

One day at work, my boss at the time asked with deep concern, "Rosemary, how are you, and how are your kids?" I told him we were all doing well, but I missed Qe and had not seen him in months. I was working hard during this time to keep myself afloat financially. So even if it crossed my mind to go visit him, it was something I immediately dismissed. He and his wife offered to help me with hotel stay and gas to go visit Qe. I was overjoyed and grateful to have a boss who cared about my family's well being. I started planning our six-hour road trip right away. Kayla and I were so excited to visit Qe. We also made plans to hang out at the beach since Qe was so close to it. This was our first official trip to the beach as a family. Life had me so bogged down with surviving from day to day that I had not even had the pleasure of simply going to the beach. Times like these often made me feel so behind in life compared to my peers, yet extremely grateful for such moments.

Little did I know how much God was ordering our steps in this spontaneous visit. Shortly after we arrived, I realized Qe was in pain. Previously I had no clue because he hadn't mentioned anything. Even when I told Qe that his sister and I were coming to visit, he didn't tell me how badly his back and shoulder were hurting. Once I discovered his pain, I went to buy an over-the-counter pain reliever and a heating pad to bring him some type of relief. He was in excruciating pain, and it alarmed my heart. When I told him he needed to go to Birmingham Children's Hospital to see his doctor, he would just say, "Yes ma'am." He didn't speak much or give me a satisfactory answer as to why he hadn't let me know he was in this sort of pain.

I didn't press him much during our time there because I wanted us to enjoy our time together as much as possible. There were times that the pain subsided enough for us to walk to the beach from our hotel (which was across the street) and hang out in the sun. The day Kayla and I were leaving, I told Qe to schedule his doctor's appointment and that I would purchase his Greyhound ticket from Mobile to Birmingham. I was grateful that God allowed me to lay eyes on my son because he had been hiding the fact that he was in pain for months. I was certain he was afraid the cancer had returned. This disease was no different from that boar that threatened the baby bear. It was as if it was looming in the background waiting to attack, and I had to be ready when it did. Just when we would think the coast was clear, it would rear its ugly head. Each time, it strengthened my determination to fight it.

I asked myself hundreds of questions as to why he handled his pain so irresponsibly. He was a couple of weeks away from turning twenty-one, but he still had more maturing to do. This was the beginning of my experience with the adult Qe with cancer. This was the hardest phase. No longer could I stay on top of things as I was used to doing because he was now handling them. Things like scheduling doctor appointments, monitoring his health up close, and conversing with doctors about plans of action were his responsibility now, not mine. Releasing him to go to college was one thing, but releasing him to handle the responsibility of his health was another.

After his appointment at Birmingham Children's Hospital, the doctors reviewed the x-rays and reported that a tiny spot previously seen on scans a couple of years prior had slightly grown. After a few years of rest from the battle, it was back. This spot had appeared on his scans from time to time but because there were no signs of growth for months, they decided to just monitor it. Doctors had even wondered at one point if it was even a tumor. Turned out that it was, and as it progressed in size it was pressing on his nerves. The pain in his shoulder would shoot down his arm into his fingers, shoulder or neck.

I went right back into mama bear mode ready to fight and claw at that which threatened my son's life. I told him he needed to move back home after this report so that he would be closer to family that could support him. Once he agreed, I began planning my trip back down to Mobile to help him move back. I didn't know how much stuff he had to move, but I was determined to make it work with what I had. At the time I drove a 2007 Montero Sport SUV. So I cleaned the trunk out, prayerfully believing his belongings could fit, and made another twelve hour round trip down to Mobile and back.

Because I had missed him, I was glad to have him back around the house again. I hated the reason he was home, but as always, I was determined to make his environment one of peace and happiness despite our circumstances. After our first visit back to Birmingham Children's Hospital with the now twenty-one-year-old Qe, doctors suggested high-intensity chemotherapy, five days a week for approximately three weeks, rest a couple of weeks, and then back at it again. It was the only thing that he hadn't done as far as treatments were concerned.

One day during the first week of scheduled chemo treatments at Children's, I was on the elevator headed to the cafeteria. There was a gentleman on the elevator who began to initiate small talk. He asked who I was with at the hospital, and I told him my son. He responded by saying he was there with his daughter. He then asked me how old my son was, and I responded that he was twenty-one. He sort of gasped as if in a little shock or maybe in amazement. He then shared with me how lucky he thought we were. His daughter also had neuroblastoma, and she was about 14. It had been so long since Qe's initial diagnosis that the aggressiveness of the disease had slipped from the forefront of my mind. So his brief expression of amazement reminded me of God's faithfulness in our journey. I got off that elevator with a refreshed gratitude because of God's miracle-working power in Qe's life.

Because I had Qe at such a young age, having him back home was like having my friend back. I enjoyed our talks about life, dreams, and financial goals. As much as I considered him a "friend" of sorts, I was always very mindful to draw a thick line between being his friend and his mother. There had to be more emphasis on *mom* than *friend* because of our closeness in age. People often complimented his respectful demeanor, but they didn't realize how much discipline and correction it took to accomplish that level of respect either.

It was great to have him back at home spending time with his siblings. It was also great to see he had his drive to succeed, and his ambition was extraordinary. He was so consumed with all the things that he wanted to do to achieve his goals that it would often leave him exhausted or indecisive, especially about which career path to choose. Sometimes he veered away from his initial goal of going into childhood oncology because he was drawn by his passion for music and entrepreneurship. These passions led him to also consider becoming a music teacher or entrepreneur.

Many times he would run all these ideas by me to ask what I thought. These conversations usually ended with him feeling overwhelmed. I believe his drive for success mirrored my own, which was driven by the desire to escape poverty and experience a better quality of life. I often chuckled at him because I knew exactly how he felt. I wrestled with my own ambition for years and tried to do ten things at once. I tried to pass on to him what my own experience had taught me. I advised him to put all his energy into learning one craft or skill, then build on that. Qe still wrestled with what to focus on, but I knew in time he would figure out his path. He had many conversations with his dad and grandmothers about his ideas as well. I'm so grateful he had multiple voices encouraging him to pursue his dreams.

Qe also had a passion to plan out his dream home. He spent his spare time either researching or watching shows about luxury homes. He would describe how his dream home would need cameras and high-tech security, which would cause me to jokingly ask, "Exactly why do you need all of this security, again?" He would watch *The World's Most Extraordinary Homes* and other similar programs on Netflix. He'd tell me how he too was going to have an extravagant home like the homeowners on the show. I loved to watch him dream and express his creativity. These conversations brought me such joy during the time that he was back home.

He still wasn't as focused as I would've liked him to be. Fighting cancer with Qe as a man was totally different than fighting cancer with Qe as a boy. When he was a kid, I had control of his surroundings. But as an adult, he would periodically hang out in environments I viewed to be detrimental to his health. Now that he was taking high-intensity chemotherapy, he needed to take extra precautions regarding his environment to avoid getting sick. During this time in his journey, he did not listen to me regarding this subject. I would get upset with him, but like any parent of a 21-year-old, you have disagreements and "out of your control" issues. I would often think in the back of my mind that we didn't have much room for error when it came to his battle with cancer.

After his first week of chemo, he told me how yucky chemo made him feel and that he didn't want to continue with the doctor's plan. He wanted to take a holistic approach. I had never heard of this method, so I was initially a bit fearful. He did ask me if I would agree with his decision. I told him that I felt uneasy about it mostly because of what I didn't know. But I saw how much this meant to him, so I began to read up on what he was sharing. It appeared he had been doing his own extensive research. There was one moment that I felt like, come on Qe, we don't have time for experiments. This was extremely uneasy for me to agree to. I decided to come on board with his plan after doing some research on my own. I knew whichever route he took, he would need his family's full support.

We were often burdened with what to keep in the diet versus what to completely kick out. To put it simply, whole foods such as vegetables, fruit, and unprocessed food was the goal. Sometimes the more we read about other people's journey to treat cancer with a holistic approach, the more burdened we became. Everyone who had been successful and become cancer-free from a holistic approach was different, but they all had one common denominator—fresh-grown and unprocessed food. Sugar was the ultimate thing to stay away from because it is what fed cancer cells. This is the basis of what we attempted to prepare for each of his meals.

Eating holistically was definitely a new approach to the journey. Now a simple trip to the grocery store was a super-complex mentally exhausting operation. I was challenged mentally, financially, and spiritually. It definitely stretched my faith.

CHAPTER FOUR

THE FIGHT WITHIN

When Qe was away at college, he had befriended a precious lady by the name of "Sweets". He worked for her to earn some extra cash on the side. Like many college students, he was trying to balance school and cover necessary expenses to make ends meet. He did various chores for her such as cleaning, cooking, and running errands. One of Sweets' crafts was making beautiful quilts by hand. Many times Qe would share with me how much he loved making quilts with her. He marveled at how beautiful the finished designs would be. I was happy to hear how much he enjoyed learning this new skill.

One day he said, "Ma, I'm going to make you a quilt!" I chuckled at his enthusiasm. I never had a quilt, let alone one that was specifically made for me. This made my heart smile, and I was very curious as to how it would turn out. After some time passed and the quilt was finished, he would try to describe to me what it looked like, but he never took a picture of it to send to me via text. I figured he wanted me to be surprised when he gave it to me in person. Because he was living in Mobile, AL, for some time after the it was completed, it eventually slipped my mind that he had made me this long-anticipated quilt. He also stopped mentioning it to me over time.

It wasn't until years later that I was reminded about Qe's quilt, and more surprisingly his reason for making it. Qe shared with Sweets that he wanted to make me a quilt to remember him by in case he didn't survive cancer. This discovery blew me away for a couple of reasons. One, I never considered that he might not make it. My faith blinded me to the "what ifs". I was only focused on Qe's complete healing. Two, the time frame in which Qe said this to Sweets was while he had been in remission for a couple of years. I thought this would have been a time death would be the furthest thing from his mind and that he would be more concerned with his ambitions and plans for his future. I now realize he may have been internally struggling with these thoughts and fears all along.

To hear Sweets tell me this brought me both joy and sorrow. It made me realize that his fight within was different from my fight for him. Whereas I was determined that as long as I fought for his life by faith he would never die from this disease, he was considering the possibility that he might die and his desire to give me something to remember him by. What a treasure! My joy was because of his expression of love toward me. My sorrow was because he was carrying the thought of facing death and leaving loved ones behind. I couldn't imagine the weight of carrying such a burden as a child or an adult.

I wondered how long he had wrestled with thoughts of leaving his family behind. I'm sure there were many battles he fought within himself that I was not privy to. I questioned myself often, but realized that God, in His faithfulness, had provided support to Qe through various friends like Sweets. These individuals were able to lend a listening ear and offer sound advice along the way. I'm sure Qe was attempting to protect me from the pain of pondering such thoughts.

Now that Qe was back home, he was the one signing his papers at doctor appointments and agreeing or disagreeing with plans for his care. He was making decisions that I had made for him his whole life, and this was difficult for me — especially if I didn't agree they were the best decisions. Qe had started a new job, and no matter how I or anyone made efforts to help him, he still wanted to work. Qe never wanted anyone bearing any of his burdens. Again, I had to step aside and allow him to make decisions for his life. This decision wasn't such a bad one, and I was actually proud to see him persevere in providing for himself and being independent. This was watching what I had preached to him his entire childhood about being a man come to life.

I've heard people say that a woman can't teach her male children how to be men. I never tried to take the place of a man in teaching my sons to be men. But I stood strong as their mother, believing that I carried the authority to teach my sons what God defined a man to be according to the scriptures. I was always very clear to both my sons that I wasn't trying to fill the void they may have experienced in our home because I was a single mother. But I was always aware of the power I had to sow seeds and speak life into their manhood. I knew and believed that I carried power as a godly parent that would profit them greatly. Realizing my weaknesses and feeling crippled by my limitations, I always prayed to God to teach my boys to be good men in this world. My desire was that they would rise above society's expectations for children of African American single moms.

His brother was released from prison around this time, and I was so happy to have all three of my children back under one roof. It had been approximately two years of just me and my Kayla-bugg. I did enjoy this time because it gave us much-needed girl time. Though Qe's battle with cancer was on the forefront of my mind, I was also trying to be there for Xzavier's rehabilitation as he dealt with the hefty prison sentence of 15 years for stealing one dollar. He was charged with first degree robbery as he was still a minor. The challenges Xzavier faced were equally heartbreaking for me.

Oftentimes, when I was at the hospital with Qe when he was younger, Xzavier was home feeling abandoned. I didn't find this out until years later. Though I left him with capable adults, his experiences were different than I expected. When Xzavier first shared this with me, I was completely shocked, and I wanted Xzavier to know how deeply this broke my heart. As I listened to Xzavier's heart, I felt crushed by the resulting emotions realizing I had failed to protect him. I fought so hard to protect all of my children from the storms of life. But I had to realize that even in my best efforts to shield my children from life's pains, I couldn't shield them from it entirely. I had to open my heart to how Qe's battle with cancer had impacted Xzavier's journey and his personal battle within.

During the time Xzavier was in prison, we had a lot of heart-to-heart conversations. It helped me to understand the fight he had to deal with within himself growing up and into his adulthood. He had gone through feeling abandoned by me and unloved by his stepfather during that time. This produced a lot of brokenness within him. Once he said to me, "Ma, I know Qe couldn't help that he had cancer, but sometimes I felt jealous and angry at him because it took so much of your attention away from me growing up." This hurt my heart to the core. I knew that I didn't love any one of my children more than the other, so for one to even have the thought that I did broke my heart. Xzavier had dealt with this internal struggle alone within himself for years.

Though I learned this when he was almost an adult, I wrestled with feeling like a failure as a mother. This caused me to come to the realization that there is only so much weight one person can carry no matter how willing they are to carry it all. I had to release the guilt and know that I did my best in that particular season. Xzavier grew to know how much I loved and supported him, but it was good to talk out the old feelings and battles he faced as a child.

Though I showed up to my family's battles like I was superwoman, I was reminded often that I wasn't. Only Jesus is a true superhero, and He lacks no strength or power.

Now that my sons were home, and my heart may have cried, "My babies!", the newly grown men reminded me on a daily basis that they were not babies anymore. They were respectful, but they had their way of seeing and doing things that caused us to bump heads now that they were young adults. I was steadfast in showing them I was the boss in my house. This resulted in some mini explosions between me and the boys during this time. These mini explosions often culminated in one or both of them storming out of the house and murmuring under their breath. All this while Kayla stood off to the side watching and shaking her head as if thinking *those boys are crazy*. We always circled back to the basics, which was our extreme love for each other. I missed all of us being together, so my heart took great delight in our movie nights, family dinners, and simply enjoying each other's company.

My main clashes of will at that time usually happened with Xzavier. He was nineteen, and we had a disagreement that resulted in me telling him, "You either do it my way because you're under my roof, or you move out and get your own place!" That disagreement resulted in both of the boys moving out. They moved to one of their friend's houses. Qe said Xzavier needed guidance, so he moved out with him to keep an eye on him. I lived in Athens, Alabama, at the time, and the boys moved to Huntsville, Alabama. It was back to just me and my sweet sidekick Kayla. Little did Qe know, the tables would be turning regarding who would need to be watched over.

It was a godsend that Xzavier was released during this time. There was a battle brewing in the background for Qe that he would need his brother. Qe's demeanor and speech began to change; his thoughts seemed disjointed as evidenced by how he frequently switched from one topic to another, with no apparent connection. I knew he was using marijuana because he said it helped with the nerve pain, but this was still out of the norm for him. Xzavier started calling me and telling me about Qe's odd behavior. He was arguing with strangers, talking about killing himself, and even laid on one of Huntsville's busiest highways, yelling that he wanted to die. It had gotten so bad, my phone was ringing off the hook almost every night because of his episodes.

It wasn't just Xzavier calling me, but people who knew I was Qe's mother. Up until that point, his dad and I rarely had consistent or healthy communication. But during this crucial time, we talked every day. We pulled together to try to figure out what was happening with our son. Xzavier felt compelled to follow Qe around to make sure he didn't get hurt by someone or hurt himself.

This time was extremely stressful. Overall, no one in our family or circle knew the source of his behavior—we could only guess. With us knowing that Qe had resorted to marijuana for help with pain relief, I was frightened that he may have gotten a hold of something that damaged his thought processes permanently. Xzavier was on a mission to find out, and if it was a controlled substance then what kind was it and where was he getting it from?

Sometimes my phone would ring between midnight and 3 am. One time, I answered and heard nothing but panting, wind, and rustling for the first 30 seconds. It was Xzavier running to another situation involving his brother. This would push me to a few minutes of panic and of course it was exhausting for Xzavier to try to explain what Qe had done or said. Once Qe had instigated an argument with a stranger, who would have seriously hurt Qe if Za wasn't there to plead with the guy to please excuse his brother. All of this felt like a nightmare. The fight for his life had mutated into a completely different beast and battleground.

I laid on my bedroom floor and cried out to God to intervene on behalf of my firstborn. I actually found myself wondering for a brief moment if this was how Qe's story would end before returning to my conviction that God wouldn't allow his journey to end this way. One day I asked Qe if I needed to take him to a drug rehabilitation center. I knew this question hit him in the gut because he wasn't used to me expressing this type of concern with such surrender. I believe Qe was shaken by what was becoming his reality and let go of whatever was causing such alarming behavior. I can only guess what type of drug it could have been. I didn't have to take him to a drug rehab because I began to see a drastic positive change in Qe's demeanor shortly after confronting him. I attribute this change to prayer and God's mercy.

CHAPTER FIVE

JUST SMILE

Almost a year and a half had passed by since Qe moved home and re-diagnosed. It seemed as if time was moving in slow motion. I guess I should say the cancer is what appeared to be moving in slow motion. As he tried to treat himself with a holistic approach, I learned so much from Qe about eating healthy and allowing food to be our medicine. We'd talk for hours about food and brainstorm about ways to reach our health goals. Kayla and I even adopted some of the same eating habits. We faced countless challenges along the way. When you overhaul your diet, grocery bills get expensive. It can also be hard to stay focused because we live in a society that heavily markets unhealthy eating and lifestyles. Meal prep was essential to maintain our new healthy eating regimen. It was our saving grace on busy days.

Qe lived so healthily and his lifestyle appeared so normal that if you didn't know he had cancer, you certainly wouldn't believe it.

Sometimes he would share with me how he was still experiencing nerve pain and headaches, but his everyday routine was that of the typical 22-year-old. Qe was working hard every day and soon moved into his own apartment. One day he introduced me to a young lady named Fiancée. She was his girlfriend. I could tell she was very special to him. I was proud to see Qe become settled and begin to build his life despite the challenges with his health looming in the background.

When his pain began to increase, I suggested that he at least look into getting radiation to speed up his healing process. I knew he wasn't sticking to the holistic diet as strictly as he should, either. Though I believe that food can be an excellent healing source for our bodies, I would have chosen the chemotherapy treatments initially given by his doctors at Birmingham Children's Hospital. Consistency in fighting against cancer is what I favored. There were times neither of us had the finances to keep up with all the different foods or nutrients needed to pursue the holistic healing approach. But I also believe there were occasions he just gave in to eating whatever he wanted, which ran counter to the regimen he was attempting to follow. He loved Popeye's Chicken. I was never against him eating what he loved. But because he chose to make his diet his primary form of treatment, it was vital for him to adhere to it because I was fully aware that his cancer couldn't just go untreated. So if I found out he was eating what he said he shouldn't, I would get upset. It felt like a ticking time bomb needing to be diffused that he was ignoring from time to time.

I was happy when he told me that he had scheduled radiation appointments with his radiation doctor. I honestly did not care what route was used to treat him. I would have tried chemo, radiation, healthy eating, and whatever else would have helped defeat this cancer if I could. Now that he was grown, I had to respect whatever decisions he made in how to treat his disease. Plus at almost every doctor's visit I was reminded that ultimately, everything was his decision; he was an adult in charge of signing the papers to authorize his treatment. But Qe would always look to me for my feedback when it came time to make decisions. I appreciated his attempts to keep me included.

Throughout the entire journey, I didn't recognize how much God was preparing, molding, and strengthening us. My focus was only to fight and beat cancer. God's view was much broader. Your viewpoint from being in the very middle of your trial is one small perspective. When God shifts your position where you are now looking at your trial from the outside, you'll have increased understanding. Whatever we face, it's always working for us a greater glory and powerful testimony.

God was preparing each of us for greater work. God had made each of us a light in such a unique way to serve His purpose of being a light to others. I was reminded of this each time the hospital staff or parents we came in contact with along the journey shared encouraging words or what they felt inspired them as they watched our journey. People have shared many testimonies with us about their faith or hope being inspired by witnessing my faith fight as a mother and his sweet smile through it all. This was a part of a greater purpose working in our life that was bigger than me just focusing on Qe's healing. God was shining through our story to everyone we came in contact with.

It felt like everyone from Birmingham Children's Hospital to Clearview Cancer Institute knew Qe by his brilliant smile and chipper demeanor. He was like a mini rock star as he strolled through the hospital or medical institute moving from clinic to x-ray and scan rooms. He was greeted with bright smiles and greetings of "Hey Q!" It may sound strange, but it even appeared that his smile was gaining more attention as time went on. His smile not only made me smile, it made everyone he came in contact with smile. It was like God was smiling at me through him, during times I felt down. Everyone would tell me how great of a job I had done raising such a polite young man and complimented his outstanding character. One day I noticed that it appeared his smile was even becoming more brilliant. He responded with a big grin, while responding seriously, "Mama, it's from all the pain I've been through." I believe that Qe's smile reflected the essence of his heart. I think it not only housed his joy but his pain. He could count on just giving you a smile if he had ever become lost for words. Qe'Vonte's smile was the common thread that held us all together throughout his journey. Anyone who encountered Qe remarked on the impact of his smile.

> I remember the day I met Qe'Vonte. I was told that I had a new student that played percussion. He came into the room and began to tell me all of the things he could play on the drums, and distinctively told me what he wanted to learn. He said, "I want to be able to play multiple instruments in the band." It was refreshing to have a student that knew what he wanted out of my class.

Qe'Vonte was always a student that worked toward his craft. He was adamant about learning the drums, but he also had a strong interest in piano. He was my "go-to" student when it came to playing different songs. I would sit down with him daily and show him different chords on the piano, and he would sit at the keyboard and practice those chords continuously. He made it easy for me to teach him new things because he was a sponge. He just learned it and kept wanting more. He was equally interested in making music as well. He also took an interest in making beats, and we often discussed new ways to create music.

He was one of my most talented students. Qe'Vonte was a very positive and optimistic student. He often came in with happiness and a smile that would light up the room. I affectionately called him "Keys to the Vonte" whenever I saw him in the hallway, lunchroom, or classroom. I would shout that out, and he would grin from ear to ear. It is something I will always remember. I grew major respect for him when he revealed to me his battle with cancer. I would have never known because of how positive he was. He never let me see him down whenever he mentioned it. He always referred to it in a "matter of fact" or "it is what it is" tone. He never felt sorry for himself.

The thing about being an educator is you never know your full reach until it is reflected back on you like a mirror. We often get caught up in the woes of education, constant

discipline issues, lesson plans, phone calls home to parents, etc. It was always great to have a student that had the ability to lift that burden even if it was for just a moment. Qe'Vonte's purpose as a student taught me to always give my all to my students. He taught me to put my feelings aside and work toward the interests and passions of my students... and for that, he will always be one of my most talented students.
—Brian Lyles *(Chapman Middle School music teacher)*

I believe my son's smile was a safe haven. It was a light that could brighten the darkest room. He told me he wanted to create a brand slogan, "Just Smile." One of his greatest desires was to encourage people to smile in the midst of hardship.

CHAPTER
SIX

BROKENNESS

Q e was receiving radiation during this time, so the treatment
plan and progress appeared to be under control. But then I
received a phone call from his girlfriend at 2 am on a Sunday
saying that Qe'vonte was unresponsive. I stumbled through the
house, praying and getting Kayla up to go with me to get to Qe as
quickly as I could. I told her to call the ambulance and that we were
on our way. I remember trying not to speed because the last thing
I needed was to be pulled over by police. Police were out heavy that
night because it was still a part of a Saturday night to some. I was
praying but shaken by the unknown.

When we pulled up at Qe's apartment, the ambulance was
there, and he was responsive. I was both relieved and alarmed at
the same time. In the middle of a conversation with his girlfriend,
Qe stopped talking, moving, or interacting. She said he just stared
into mid-air.

When I arrived, he was talking to the EMTs. They assumed his unresponsiveness had to do with the tumors he had on his spine, but they were unsure. Qe'vonte decided to not go with the ambulance that night and to follow up with his doctor the next business day. Many times health professionals were puzzled by Qe's cancer or symptoms, and we found it better to stick with the doctors who were most familiar with his medical background.

As a result of he and I clashing several times over what treatment should look like, I had taken the back seat concerning his care. He'd had full liberty to make decisions regarding his health for a couple of years now. It was both scary and uncomfortable for me because nothing about our situation was ordinary. In nearly every decision, we had to factor in his cancer diagnosis and current health status. This often made things more complicated than they normally would be. I had relinquished my authority to fully place his care in his hands. He was grown and I had to adapt to only coaching him from the sidelines.

As much as I wanted to stay on the sidelines and respect his choices, I knew I had to work my way back to having more input and control in the decision making process. After this episode I dared him to get in my way. I refused to watch his life slip away because of poor choices. Qe was selfless, strong-minded, and very mindful of not being a burden to anyone. I lovingly reassured him that managing cancer was too great of a task for anyone to tackle by themselves. I made it clear to him that no matter a person's age, cancer is an illness that requires a support system. It was important to me to let him know that I fully respected his manhood even though in my heart, he was still my sweet boy.

Monday morning, I called and left messages at the center where he was receiving radiation. I questioned nurses and left messages for the doctor about the unresponsive episode. I reached out to friends for help to buy food and supplements to support Qe's holistic regimen. At this time, we only knew of two to three tumors on his spine, and it didn't make sense for him to become unresponsive. The paramedics also referred to it as seizure-like activity.

At first, the response from a nurse that returned one of my messages was that the doctor said this episode wasn't related to his cancer at all—that cancer would not cause such an event. But I pressed for them to reevaluate and do an MRI. I was uncomfortable with just blowing this off as something not severe. I've learned that we know our bodies best and need to act on symptoms we know aren't normal because it could be detrimental toward preventing something fatal. Qe'Vonte had been experiencing numbness in his legs for a few months. The tumors on his spine had caused some nerve damage. With that knowledge alone, we could not afford to be dismissive. The center finally scheduled him an appointment the following week for an MRI.

I also became aware of how much pain Qe had been in over the past few weeks. I wanted him to find some sort of rest and relief… something like a vacation away from everything. He told me a year or so prior, about a place where people with cancer went and sought rest and a holistic approach to healing. He expressed his desire to be able to go to something like this, but we couldn't afford it. I began to do some research to find such a place to surprise Qe with some time away to rest and recoup. I was excited to find a place by the name of Wildwood Lifestyle Center that was only a few hours away. I was determined to give this to him as a gift, so I started a GoFundMe to raise money for him to go. He was so excited about the opportunity.

During this time Qe loved going to physical therapy. He had to eventually stop working because of the pain and stiffness he was experiencing in his legs and back, along with severe headaches. I believe physical therapy gave him a sense of purpose and motivation to keep moving. One day when he was on his way back from PT, he blacked out while driving and hit a curb. This incident took place the following week after he had become unresponsive. Family and friends warned him that it wasn't a good idea for him to drive, but this was his strong will at work as he fought to stay independent. By God's grace, he was protected from being in a deadly car accident. He thought he had simply dozed off, but he had actually blacked out again. His dad, his girlfriend, and I convinced him to stop driving altogether and to let us transport him back and forth to all appointments. I knew he hated losing the independence of driving. It was as if the things he worked hard to accomplish were slowly being stripped from him.

I was bothered that his MRI was scheduled so many days away from his initial episode. In my heart, I knew something serious was happening that we did not have full knowledge of. On the Sunday before the appointment, I was led to go and check on Qe. I was tired that day and wanted to go home and relax. But as I vacillated between going to his house or going home, the urgency grew. I texted him, asking how he was doing, and he said he was in some pain and wanted to come over to my house to get some rest.

It had become harder for him to rest, and he wanted to sleep on his sister's memory foam mattress.

When I arrived, he loaded up, and we were on our way to my house. I noticed that his pupils were uneven, and he looked so unlike himself that I made a u-turn and took him straight to the emergency room instead of waiting for the scheduled MRI appointment. The ER scan revealed a tumor at the base of his brain that was blocking spinal fluid from flowing properly. The excess fluid caused pressure on his brain, which caused Qe'Vonte's blackouts, headaches, and sporadic pains throughout his body. Madison Hospital transferred him by ambulance to Huntsville Hospital, where a neurosurgeon could further evaluate.

Though we laughed and joked that day in the emergency room after being given the results, I was deeply distressed by the news. We had never faced this level of disturbance with his health. I was shaken, but preparing myself to go into fighting mode. Qe didn't seem to be worried, but I'm sure he inwardly had his own concerns. The plan was for Kayla to ride with him in the ambulance, and I would meet them there. She was Qe's right hand. I was always tempted to feel like I had to shield her from the pain of watching him go through all of this. But I knew that we both didn't want to be anywhere other than by his side. I reached out to close friends and my pastor that I often drew strength from to petition for their prayers. They were always there during my most significant times of opposition. Leaning on the Word of God, my pastor, church family, and many faith-filled friends was where I regained my strength and focus to keep fighting.

As a boxer fighting in the ring periodically needs time to rally in their corner with their trainer and support system, so did I. I went to this corner quite often over the next few months. Qe was admitted to the Neuro-Intensive Care Unit (NICU) upon arrival at Huntsville Hospital. By the second day, his cries of pain morphed into earnest prayers. The problems he was experiencing were coming from the spinal fluid backed up in the brain. This caused the brain to receive incorrect signals that communicated various places on the right side of his body were experiencing sharp stabbing-like pains. Qe's situation was complicated by the fact that he was receiving no pain medication. If he received pain medication, it could cause him to become lethargic and interfere with identifying any new episodes. It was heartbreaking for me to see him endure this level of pain without pain relief.

When Qe started praying out loud, he confessed things that he felt he had done wrong. He would say, "Lord, I'm so sorry for taking life for granted... I'm sorry for all of my sins. Please forgive me—I've acted so foolishly." He would pray out loud as if I wasn't in the room. Sometimes he'd just start crying as if in deep sorrow. As a parent that is a follower of Jesus Christ, one of your number one desires is to see your children have a personal relationship with the Lord. Everyone has their own unique path of how their relationship begins and how their faith is further cultivated. I saw the beauty of God's grace and the humility of my son's heart. I loved that he called out to the Lord for himself, but my heart ached for him. As he was being broken, my heart was breaking for him.

I can't say that my son didn't have a relationship with Christ before this point because only God knows. But I do know that I had witnessed much of what I was hearing him repent for. And that I was observing him come to some level of a breaking point and surrender to God. Those of us who have received Jesus as our Lord and Savior all have something that led us to the foot of the cross. Something was the catalyst to the humble acceptance of the fact that we needed Jesus. Maybe the brunt of Qe's surrender came from him feeling helpless in his battle with cancer, and that brought him to this beautiful breaking point before God. Maybe it was the excruciating pain he was in. No matter how or why we come, Jesus just wants us to *come*. Whatever drives us there isn't the most important thing. The most important thing is that we lay our burdens at the feet of the cross in complete surrender.

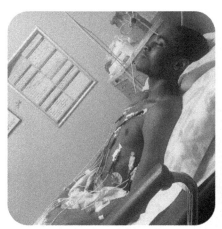
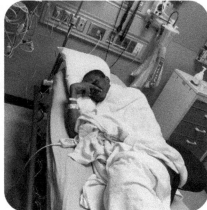

CHAPTER
SEVEN

THE DARK ROOM

My pain seemed to parallel his. If he was uncomfortable, I was uncomfortable; if he was sleepless, I was sleepless. His physical and emotional distress became the source of my physical and emotional distress. I felt like my faith was being put on trial. After the MRI at Huntsville hospital, doctors told us that in addition to the tumor found at the base of his neck, there were additional spots of tumors found throughout his brain. The impact of this news felt like a wrecking ball to the chest, and somehow, someway, I was still standing.

The doctor's main focus was to get the spinal fluid flowing and stop the build-up in Qe's brain. The pressure in his brain caused sporadic pains throughout the right side of his body. The first few days, he continuously tossed and turned. Each time he moaned in pain, my soul ached for him. Each time, I searched for comfort in the Word of God. I related to the suffering of Mary the mother of

Jesus like never before. I imagined how she must have felt as she watched her son be punished and suffer such pain for the sins of the world. I knew these were two totally different scenarios, but in some way, it brought me comfort to know that my pain could be relatable to any mother's pain in the present or in the past. I wondered if the pain I felt was even close to what she must have experienced as she watched her son's suffering. Mary also being a young virgin girl having a baby, her life went from innocence to insults, much like my own. She overcame obstacles of being a teen mom, only to later watch her baby experience such agony. I found comfort in these parallels within our stories.

The neurosurgeon and her team came up with a plan to surgically place a shunt in Qe'Vonte's brain. This hollow tube would drain the excess cerebrospinal fluid to his stomach. We would then follow up with more radiation a few weeks after discharge. Once the decision was made, surgery was scheduled just a few days later. A doctor came in one day to check on Qe, and began to discuss his MRI results. He also began to rattle off what he believed to be Qe's options at this point. If I hadn't been listening closely, I could have missed that he mentioned hospice as an option. Just hearing the word hospice associated with Qe shook my inner being. There was no way I was accepting that Qe had reached the end of his life, and I definitely had not reached the end of my fight for him. So I quickly assured the doctor that we would choose every option available while I strongly dismissed the option of hospice. Qe was listening intently with little to no verbal response.

Later on, I decided to reach out to a dear friend of mine that I knew Qe looked up to and simply adored. I also respected her as a powerful woman of God. She was his Bible study teacher during his teen years and was my pastor's daughter. I felt the need to reach outside myself for help in keeping Qe's spirit lifted. Though he was smiling, I could tell he was slightly bothered. Jemeana gladly stopped by the hospital that day with her husband Demond. I left her in the room to give them privacy because I also wanted to provide Qe the space to confide in her in case he needed it. I knew that he might have things on his heart that he may have not wanted to share with me and his dad. I used this time to go downstairs and grab a bite to eat. When I came back to his room, Qe was crying and thanking God in a way I had never heard before. He and Jemeana were holding hands and as she was praying, his voice was lifted in praise to God. I was ecstatic to hear the sound of joy and praise from my son. A few days prior, I watched him in deep sobs of repentance which now appeared to be turned into tears of joy. Witnessing God doing a work in Qe's heart was such a blessing to me.

Friends and family came to the hospital the day of his surgery to support and be there for Qe. There was a large community praying with us. As I was in his room to assist with whatever prep was needed before the surgery, we joked around and laughed. We had high hopes of a great successful outcome, and we discussed what he would like to eat after surgery. This was one of our happy places and main topics before all of his surgeries or procedures. Because the usual protocol is that you can't eat after midnight before the scheduled procedure, Qe usually said that he was starving even before they could come to get him for surgery. The question of how soon he could eat was at the top of his priority list. Qe absolutely loved food. I would usually ask him what he wanted to eat after his procedures because of the joy that food brought him. As soon as the nurses took him off to surgery, I'd get him whatever he wanted and have it ready for him when he was able to eat. As so many other times before, I watched him being rolled away from me to a room I was restricted from entering and my heart would break again. We would smile at each other and he'd say, "Love you Ma," and I would respond, "I love you too son." I'd watch him until he was completely out of my sight, and tears would begin to fall.

A few hours later we were notified that his surgery went well, and now we were waiting to hear further details from the neurosurgeon. Family sat in the waiting room as we waited for the doctor to come and talk to us. The doctor came in and greeted us with a huge smile, and began to share the details of the surgical process. She was going on about how great everything went with the surgery, but I zeroed in on the sadness I saw hiding behind her smile. We all gave a sigh of relief to know how successful the surgery was, but I still felt bothered. I could see beyond her words. She took a breath and began to say that even with the surgery relieving the pressure from Qe's brain, that she and her team expected him to have six months to live at most. And if cancer cells were in the spinal fluid (that was now running down to his stomach), Qe might only have a few weeks left.

When I first heard those words, it was like that same wrecking ball had taken its third swing to my heart. I stood up (for some strange reason), and then my legs gave way as I fell to the floor. It was like a dam of emotions had burst within me. I cried from the depths of my soul. The pain felt unbearable. As I reached within to gain composure, I searched for God, like a person in a dark room feeling for a light switch. After I was able to compose myself a bit, I stood up and shook the doctor's hand. I felt the need to apologize for becoming so emotionally unraveled, and she assured me that no apologies were necessary. She then apologized for having to deliver such devastating news. My friend Mary Alice stood by my side comforting me. I looked around and no one else was in the room. My heart panicked for Kayla. I wanted to get to her quickly. I didn't know what frame of mind this may have thrust her into. I knew I had to believe in God's ability to heal above all. But I had never had to have faith for something of this magnitude, so I was searching hard for God's leading and comfort.

After finding Kayla, making sure she was okay, and reassuring her everything was going to be fine, I stepped outside to call my pastor. I was deeply torn and unsure of what to reach for in my faith. Not only did I feel like I was in a dark room grasping for the light switch, it felt like the darkness was growing even darker by the minute. By now, I was wondering if the dark room I felt I was in even had a light switch at all. What light could I find in this darkness that my soul was experiencing? I felt like I couldn't see as clearly as usual and my strength felt so small. I hid this as much as I could from loved ones. I didn't want anyone to be misled into thinking that I was lacking faith or giving up. My inner conviction to be a light and example as a follower of Jesus Christ has always weighed heavily on the forefront of my heart. I only wanted to reflect that which I thought would bring God the greatest glory. In the midst of my pain, I pulled on God's strength to continue to speak life to my children and those who circled around me.

In that conversation with my pastor, one of the many profound things she said to me was "Wherever there is life, there is God." This statement gave me the strength to trust and believe that God could and would heal Qe. I kept repeating this over and over to myself, especially when I felt doubt wanting to creep in. It served as my initial reminder that as long as my son had breath in his body, God was able to heal him completely. I saw how much God was with Qe. He was still full of so much life and his smile expressed that more than a million words. Because Qe was still recovering from the surgery and tired, we all agreed to not share what the doctor said about his possible life expectancy. Even the doctors agreed to wait until after he was discharged and returned for his first followup visit to share this news. My pastor's encouraging words gave me strength while I was still processing the disheartening news.

Later the same day, as I was sitting outside the hospital with friends and family, I became overwhelmed with emotion again. I felt like the weight of the entire 15-year journey of fighting for my son's life had come center stage to lay claim to the core of why I fought so hard. I had consistently claimed that he would live a long life. And now I was faced with foreboding thoughts of death. All I wanted was for Qe to live and not die, as it is written in God's Word. I felt like a victor up until the point when I began to question if I could still believe in the face of such adversity.

As I sat with close friends and family circled around the table, I felt my determination crumbling. I can vividly remember the facial expressions of each individual that sat around that table in complete silence. I burst into tears again, overcome by so many motherly emotions, not the least of which was the fear of losing my son. Boniechia got up to comfort me, embracing my head in her arms just as any big sister would embrace her little sister. I felt like I was coming apart at the seams. It was a time for us all to process and come to terms with the situation.

I made the choice to hold on to the words my pastor spoke and I focused on the word of God despite how I felt. I wondered deep inside whether I had enough faith to overcome and reverse what the doctors' expectations were. Various testimonies of other miraculous things that had been done in other people's lives were shared with me, and I latched on to hope with everything I had. After hearing or reading about them, I knew God would do it for Qe. I girded myself in my most holy faith to expect healing for him even in such a dark hour. After the surgery, Qe was so much happier because the sharp pains had subsided. This gave me great joy! I would overhear him telling friends or family that he was grateful I took him to the emergency room when I did. My heart was overjoyed. This was refreshing to hear after shifting back to the frontlines to fight alongside him. Because I never wanted him to feel like I was overstepping him.

The success of his surgery gave us the hope and strength needed to keep moving forward. But I still wrestled in the dark room of my mind as I was searching for God's direction and assurance. I was horrified whenever I thought of how Qe would react to the news that the doctors didn't expect him to live much longer. The very thought crushed me every moment, but I continued to pray and trust that God was in control. A day after surgery, the ambulance came to transport Qe to Clearview Cancer Institute for the resumption of his radiation.

Before Qe's surgery, my pastor came to visit him, and it was a visit I'll never forget. We fervently prayed and made faith declarations. One of the things she repeated over and over to Qe was, "You gotta tell it son!" He was exclaiming it as well, "I gotta tell it Pastor!" They were both joyously declaring that he would soon tell all that God had miraculously done and would do for him. By faith, he set his expectations to live and to tell his testimony. My pastor led him through a prayer of rededicating his life to Christ. He wept and praised God in that hospital bed for the second day in a row.

As a mother who had diligently prayed and believed that her children would love and serve God, this was monumental and the most beautiful thing I could witness. God's presence filled the room, and we all gave God praise. God was moving in ways that reassured me that He was working out a greater purpose. I began to see something blooming in my darkness that was more purposeful than what was causing the darkness, which was my son's true salvation.

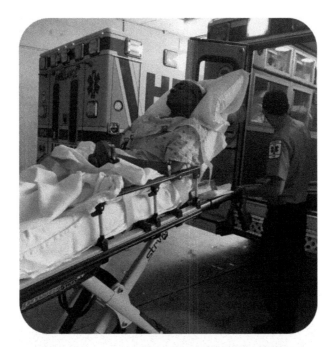

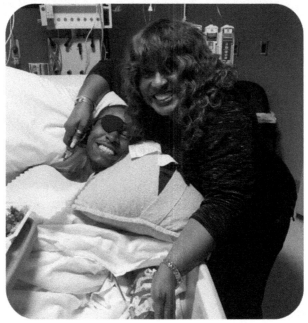

CHAPTER
EIGHT

ONLY BELIEVE

Before Qe's discharge from the hospital, messages began to pour in from our family, church members, and friends all around the city. I had spent so much time alone in those early years at Birmingham Children's Hospital that fighting alone while praying to God had become my default and norm. Now it felt like God sent people to help us right as the need appeared. Before I even realized the need, God provided. It was as if the need and the answer showed up at the same time. My friends were like angels sent from heaven. I had girded myself for the fight so many times in the past while being alone, I didn't realize how much I would need the help of others this time, but God did.

Because Qe had been living on his own, and things were moving so fast in the hospital, I didn't realize I had to prepare the extra room at my house for him. We decided he would move back home after discharge so I could help him through the healing process. Along with everything moving rapidly, there was a lot of information to digest and make decisions about. My angel-like friends recognized the need for the room to be prepared before he was to come home from the hospital, and they took charge of not only supplying the needed furniture and setting it up, but also surprising me with a mini house makeover. Meals and groceries were organized and brought to our house weekly, and rides were lined up to help me get him back and forth to radiation appointments, etc. These were just some of the countless acts of love we were blessed to receive. Loved ones and the body of Christ showed up exponentially over the following months in expressing their great love toward my family.

After Qe's discharge from the hospital, I leaned on God to help me stay strong, and I held on to the Word of God. I grabbed for hope, and I fed that hope to all of my children like it was the food they needed to survive. It was important to me that his siblings had hope and could see God's hand of provision and love in this process. I often read and confessed the promises of God to encourage myself. I knew that healing was the will of God for my son's life. It's important when believing God for a miracle that you surround yourself with faith-filled people and truth from God's word. I had believed God would heal my son from the time he was eight years old. God always granted my requests which resulted in the cancer going into remission. But believing in this season was more challenging than ever before.

Qe was so happy to come home. His grandmother from Chicago had come to be by his side. He called her "GG." They always had a special relationship. Robert (his dad) and grandmother Lonnie

(GG) came to help Qe any way they could. He especially looked forward to his grandmother's cooking. Qe always had a large appetite, and he was looking forward to eating meals that weren't takeout or hospital food. But when he got home he didn't have the appetite or energy that we'd expected. He laid in the bed almost all day and night. He didn't want anything to eat, and when he did eat, he ate very small portions. After a few days of this, I was greatly disturbed. He had become so lethargic and limp that he couldn't sit up for more than 15 minutes before he'd go back to lying down in bed. That progressed to the point of him not wanting to get out of the bed at all. By now, the trip that I had anxiously planned for him to go to Wildwood was cancelled because he had become too weak.

He lost his appetite completely, and lost over 10 pounds. This was alarming because he was already a small guy. I was terribly afraid that he was dying right before my eyes. At one point, I had to walk outside away from him and Kayla because I was overwhelmed with emotions. I stood on the curb as I looked up toward the sky with tears in my eyes, fervently petitioning God to save my son's life. I kept thinking about the time limit the doctors gave him. It was daunting and challenging to my faith, but I chose to believe God for the miraculous. The feeling of being in a dark room had been looming over me ever since I received the report that the cancer had spread to his brain. At that time, Qe was still unaware of the news from the doctors, and he still appeared too weak to take such a blow.

During this time Xzavier wasn't home much at all, and I don't think he was taking Qe's struggle with cancer well. I assumed he was the type of person to isolate himself during trials. I knew that this was his method of dealing with the hardship. But this awareness of his coping didn't prevent me from being disappointed and frustrated with him. It was only natural that I would expect him to help with Qe'Vonte because he was the second oldest. This quite often led to Kayla stepping up in his place. Wanting to protect her from feeling unduly burdened at her young age, I tried to assume as much responsibility for Qe's care myself. In addition, there were tons of people showing up in a tremendous number of ways, offering help where they could. It was like God had sent angels disguised as friends to my address.

The next morning after I had prayed fervently, Qe's condition was unchanged. I lay in my bed, feeling completely depleted of strength and void of direction. Over all the years that I had prayed, believed, and trusted God, he had never gotten this sick. It was hard to see past the doctor reports and Qe's declining state. I knew that God was with me, but the pain of watching my son's battle made me question God's plan. My grief was great, and the darkness felt like it was closing in. Qe's illness was progressing, and I found myself reaching for hope and healing like never before. I lay in bed and told God, "I need your strength to fight and your direction on how to proceed." I poured out my need to Him in that hour because I felt that I was at the end of my rope and didn't know what else to do. In that moment I was reminded of a local natural store called Creative Healing that Qe had started going to at one point in his holistic journey. It was like God turned on a light bulb. I jumped up and immediately went to Ms. Linda's (the owner) to ask for help.

My first concern was that Qe had stopped eating. I figured if I could help him get his appetite back, it would lead to him regaining his strength. I left Creative Healing with some glutamine and Probiotics 500 which would help with nausea and gut restoration. Qe had gone through several radiation treatments prior to surgery, which could have contributed to his loss of appetite. I also got some Essiac Tonic, Chlorofresh, and some vegetables to juice. These items were the weapons I had in my hands to help me fight. I knew how much he loved natural approaches to healing, so I was excited to show him what I had gotten to hopefully give him strength.

It was amazing! After a day or so of juicing fresh fruit and vegetables along with the supplements, Qe's entire demeanor had changed. He could now sit up for a few hours at a time and eventually worked up to being able to sit up an entire day. I knew that God had prompted me to go to Creative Healing as I prayed for direction and strategy to fight. His appetite was much better, but he hadn't eaten much for a couple of weeks, so he couldn't take in a large quantity of food. However, we were excited about what seemed to be this immediate turnaround in Qe's healing process. It uplifted me so much to see him laughing and having a good time with family and friends again. Everyone was full of hope that he could make it past this now that he had regained strength.

I felt a renewed sense of strength and was ready to continue fighting. He had a followup appointment with the radiation doctor fast approaching. I knew they would tell Qe their thoughts on how long they expected him to live. Every part of me hated this for him. How would he react? Would this crush any belief he had that he could be healed? Would this cause him to stop fighting? Would he be terrified? Questions raced through my mind, making my heart heavy for him. I chose to focus on what the Word of God promised about healing so that I could be strong for him.

I focused on stories that built my faith, such as Jairus falling at Jesus' feet begging Him to heal his daughter because she was dying. I was Jairus, begging the Lord to heal my child because the doctors said that he was dying. Jairus' daughter even died, and Jesus' only reply to him was, "Do not be afraid; only believe," and Jesus raised her from the dead. This gave me hope and increased my faith in the midst of my own darkness, and I focused on only believing. I was fully persuaded that my son would receive a miracle. Like the woman with the issue of blood had her issue for twelve years, it had been 15 years since Qe was first diagnosed. I could relate to the weariness she must have felt, yet she pressed toward Jesus. Lord knows, I can't even imagine how Qe must have felt being the one having to actually deal with the illness.

Qe, like her, had reached a point that there was nothing else doctors could do. But because of her faith to press past the crowd and reach out to touch the hem of Jesus' garment with the intent that she would receive healing, she did. These stories strengthened my faith in the healing power of Jesus Christ and reminded me that Qe was already healed by His stripes. If they could receive healing, so could Qe. So I stood on these biblical truths. However, just as these individuals had their own unique story and miraculous encounters with Christ, God was building Qe's own unique and miraculous story.

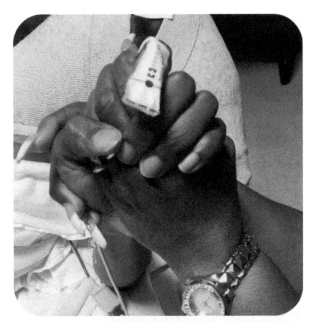

CHAPTER
NINE

AT THE FEET OF JESUS

Everyone's heart was glad to see Qe's strength returning. My schedule became a balance between daily juicing, organizing visits, frequent radiation appointments, physical therapy, and balancing work. Kayla was helping Qe stay on schedule with taking his medicines and supplements. The new radiation schedule was five days a week for approximately three weeks, and physical therapy two to three times a week. I was also trying to maintain going to work every day. This is where our community of family and friends stepped in to help carry the load and became known as Team Qe'Vonte. I couldn't have successfully balanced life in this season without their support.

Because he had been exposed to so much radiation already, more radiation was a bit scary for me because now they were radiating his entire head along with a couple of more spots on his spine. His legs had been numb since March, and it was now June.

The small spots on his spine were thought to be the root of the numbness he was experiencing. I had never heard of anyone receiving radiation this extensively, and I was concerned about the possible side effects. But my desire to see him get well outweighed my fears. These treatments were intended to prevent symptoms from making Qe'vonte uncomfortable at what they now viewed as the end of his life. Medical professionals made sure to communicate to us that these treatments were not expected to bring complete healing, but I was persistent in believing they would eventually bring about the healing I continued to pray so desperately for.

On the day of his first followup appointment, he was surrounded by family and friends, all bracing ourselves for the news that would be shared with him that day. By this point, I had a singular focus on God performing a miracle for Qe. It was also a few days away from his birthday, so in the background I was thinking about how I could bring joy to his world after all he had been through in the recent months. As the doctor entered the room, Qe greeted him with the biggest smile and sweetest demeanor. The doctor began by reviewing reports already shared with us by the doctors at the hospital which led to the heartbreaking news.

The radiation doctor, Dr. Childs, had known our family since Qe was about twelve years old and had to go through radiation. Now here it was almost ten years later. Qe had to undergo treatments again under his supervision. I can't imagine how hard it must have been for Dr. Childs to break this news to Qe. He was his patient, but they had also become friends. After a brief review, he proceeded by saying to Qe, "You know I always promised you that I would always be 100% honest with you." Qe smiled, nodded, and said "Yes sir, you did." Dr. Childs continued to say "due to the spread of the cancer throughout your brain, you may have six months to live at the most and two weeks to live if there were any cancer cells in the spinal fluid being drained by shunt." Qe sat there quietly for a second, then smiled and said, "Ok."

He thanked the doctor for everything, and tears began to flow down his cheeks. Then he immediately wiped his tears and assured all of us that he was okay. He appeared to be a little speechless which I'm sure he was because of the shocking report. Our only option medically was to continue with radiation treatments that were merely to offer him comfort, not a cure. The doctors didn't see anything else they could do to completely cure Qe of cancer. Even still, I chose to fight the good fight of faith. I believed that we all have the choice to believe in God's abilities or not to believe. I chose to believe despite everything that was going on around me. I set my focus on believing despite the odds.

Going against the grain to believe God had become my norm and essential necessity for obtaining a miracle. Having walked this faith journey for 15 years, I saw God carry my son up to this point. God had never forsaken us. Considering the other personal battles I had fought by faith and seen God move miraculously, I couldn't give up now. Having always respected the medical professionals' advice and wisdom, I chose to put my faith in God first, looking to the One that created the knowledge that they studied to obtain. We all went home that day from the doctor's office with heavy hearts and some level of determination to fight in the presence of our fears. While I was choosing to be strong for Qe, I didn't realize until later how much he was trying to be strong for me and shield me from his burdens.

I asked Qe if it was ok for me to put together a birthday gathering for him. He shrugged his shoulders as if saying why not, and he said, "Yeah, Ma…that's straight," accompanied by his galactic smile. I could only imagine how exasperating the last couple of months had been for him. I never wanted Qe'Vonte to feel alone in his battle. I wanted him to feel loved and not abandoned. This was just my mother's intuition, not anything that Qe had outrightly expressed to me. But he later admitted (after the party) that he didn't know so many people loved him. I did whatever I felt it took for him to know he was loved, not just by me, but many. I got to moving quickly because it was only a week away.

After expressing this to Boniechia, she and her husband Kris gladly opened their home up for us to throw him a pool party that he would never forget. They had a big beautiful swimming pool that the family hadn't had the chance to break in yet, and this was the perfect opportunity. I was so grateful to see how excited and eager friends and family were to come and celebrate Qe. He was definitely worth celebrating and loving on. Kris and Boniechia worked hard behind the scenes, graciously preparing their space for the celebration.

Though I hadn't accepted the doctor's report because I chose to believe God for the miraculous, it didn't keep me from feeling even more grateful for his life after what threatened to take it away. So this birthday felt especially special to me. This party was another way to express our joy in the midst of our challenging times. The day of his birthday was not only joyous to him but to all who celebrated with us. He was so happy, and my heart was happy because of it.

My beloved friend Toya photographed and captured our moments that day. When I created the album of his birthday pictures, I was inspired to entitle it with the scripture reference from Exodus 12:14..."And this day shall be unto you for a memorial." I imagined our future sharing how we had been through such trying times and telling nations of how God miraculously healed Qe'Vonte. We celebrated what was projected to be his last birthday with faith and joy in the hope of our God. That it would be a memorial of God's goodness and miraculous healing power.

Qe shared his birthday, June 21st, with the first day of summer. What a perfect day for the day of his birth. I often called him my Sonshine because he brightened my day and energized my fight for his life as well as my own. His gift of smile illuminated his environment like the sun on the brightest summer day. Everything I associated with the summertime reflects Qe'Vonte's spirit: fun-loving, playful, happy, full of love, and exuberant! His smile and personality could light up my darkest room. What was blooming in my darkness was him choosing to smile in the midst of his greatest pain.

After enjoying such a beautiful birthday gathering, I started to focus on what more I could do to fight. I contacted St. Jude and his childhood doctor at Birmingham Children's Hospital.

Birmingham scheduled an appointment for us to come but expressed there weren't any available options to help Qe outside of chemo. There was even strong uncertainty about that because of the progression of the cancer. His childhood doctor, Dr. Hilliard gave us some suggestions, and one of them was to reach out to Memorial Sloan Kettering in New York. I grabbed for any line of hope, so I immediately contacted Memorial Sloan Kettering to begin the process of getting Qe there. This turned out to be quite an extensive process, and I was becoming frustrated because I knew time was of the essence. When St. Jude and a doctor that specializes in brain tumors at the University of Alabama Hospital at Birmingham both replied that there was nothing either of them could do as well, I became distraught.

While at work, I was juggling calls from nurses and doctor offices regarding Qe. I'd often step away to handle the call and go back to my desk as if I wasn't dealing with the complex mazes and massive issues I was actually facing. When I received the calls that neither St. Jude or the neuro-specialist in Birmingham could help us, I broke down crying. I had to leave work early that day because I couldn't pull myself together. I didn't want my children to see me this way either, so I drove up and down the highway to pray and cry. I talked to God about how the doors that had previously given us hope were now closing. I felt that we were running out of time and that I was backed into a corner with no discernible way out. It seemed obvious my only option was to trust God even more.

After this, I realized that I could only focus truly on God and the little we were able to do at home with a holistic lifestyle. I began to rest all of my expectations fully on God's ability. I gave thanksgiving and praise in advance to express my faith to God for the miracle of Qe'Vonte's healing. As Qe and I would always have our talks about our dreams and goals for the future, I would still talk about these things to show God and Qe that I wasn't giving up. I made sure to continuously speak life. There wasn't a doctor that felt there was hope for Qe to make it, and though this was devastating, I couldn't give up on maintaining a ferocious faith.

During a time that I was in the chapel at the hospital praying when Qe was there, the Lord placed a passage of scripture on my heart:

Then great multitudes came to Him, having with them the lame, blind, mute, maimed, and many others; and they laid them down at Jesus' feet, and He healed them. —Matthew 15:30 (NKJV)

Reading this passage was monumental for me. It molded my faith and trust in the Lord throughout the upcoming months. This multitude of people were carrying seriously ill people who were in need of healing to the feet of Jesus. The people being carried were probably their loved ones, their neighbors, and some may have even been strangers. After being laid at His feet, Jesus healed them. This passage of scripture gave me the peace and direction I needed. I knew I had to bring Qe to Jesus and lay him at His feet. Every time I prayed, praised, or rendered thanksgiving, I pictured me laying my son in the safest and surest place of peace and healing, the feet of Jesus. It took faith to lay my sweet boy at Jesus' feet when my logical understanding couldn't see how things would work out. I had to walk by faith and not by sight.

CHAPTER
TEN

A New Walk

O ne of my frustrations was getting Qe to communicate when he needed help or if he felt symptoms worsening. Helping him without offending him was always heavy on my heart. Qe would get stronger for a few weeks, but soon his walking would become more unsteady. After finishing three weeks of radiation, the MRI revealed that there was another small tumor on his spine. It was located in the upper middle part of his back, and suspected to be the source that was impairing his walking. Consequently, they scheduled another three weeks of radiation for that particular spot. Kayla and I became more glued to his side because of our concern for him falling. He would still attempt to move with the same speed and tenacity as if he wasn't struggling, which caused us to be even more nervous. He would sternly tell us, "I got this!" or "I'm ok," sending a strong message that he did not feel that he needed our help. I not only knew that his mind and will had not accepted the reality of what was happening to his body, but that this was also his way of fighting.

I no longer got a full night's sleep, but slept in spurts off and on in both the day and night. I was watching him like a hawk because of his lack of communication. I didn't want to be blindsided by any more discouraging surprises in his health, especially if it could be avoided. I knew that he was up at all times of night as well. Almost every time I walked past his room, whether to peek in on him or just passing by, I would see his toes wiggling as he was lying in bed. He fought the numbness in his legs for months by going to physical therapy and the gym. Qe would do these extreme workouts that had us concerned that he was putting too much on his body. He was also doubling up on whatever he did at physical therapy. One day I decided to mention that I noticed how much I saw him wiggling his toes, and he told me that he did it because it was always on his mind that there may come a day he wouldn't be able to. I was speechless and could only smile and nod in my admiration of his fighting spirit. This also revealed that his internal battle was growing.

He soon let down his guard and allowed us to help him after a couple of scares where he almost fell. I grew tired of feeling like I was walking on eggshells in his presence. I let him know that I was only trying to be preemptive against further injury. His dad would assure him as well that he needed to allow us to help him. I could tell by his change in attitude that he accepted our help with a new mindset. He gradually stopped pushing us away and eventually grew to be able to joke around and make light of the situation. I believe this was his way of coping when things became uncomfortable or overwhelming.

Watching him as he attempted to function normally while "normal" was being slowly stripped away caused me to feel a level of grief I'd never experienced. I took many drives alone just to cry because it broke me inside. We both fought the idea of a walker as long as we could. Even so, I soon realized that I'd rather have him use a walker which granted him some form of independence than to go without one. I was still going to work, and I was much more comfortable with the fact that he had a walker to lean on than not. As God graced me to see through a different set of eyes, I was able to share with Qe and it helped his outlook on the transition as well. One day we were sitting on the couch side by side, and he grabbed my hand. He said, "Mom, I'm scared…I'm so scared," with tears beginning to fall down his face. I squeezed his hand with every bit of confidence I had in who I knew God to be, and I promised him with great assurance that he was going to be just fine. I can't describe the amount of strength that surged through me to fight even harder after hearing my son speak these words. I felt like I could move mountains and whatever else stood in his way.

Using a walker, like many things throughout this journey, was not easy for us to embrace in the beginning because it went against our will for him to get better. In addition, it is just hard when you've been independent of such things your whole life. It was enlightening to embrace our new reality without allowing it to erode our faith. Sharing these perspectives with my children seemed to help us all walk through the inevitable with grace. Earlier in my faith walk, I would have felt that accepting the need for a walker would have meant I didn't really believe in what God could do. I thank God for the progression of my growth and how

He helped me to stop leaning on my own understanding. My mindset changed to not look at the walker as a sign of defeat but a bridge to victory because he would not need it one day.

At times Qe would be walking while holding the walker slightly above the floor. He was still fighting for his legs, and he didn't want to use it if he was strong enough to walk on his own. I laughed so hard the first time I saw him do this because it caught me off guard to see him walking with the walker midair never touching the ground. Qe's quirky resilient personality would make me chuckle many times, and this was one of those moments. He smirked at me while appearing amused that he unintentionally made me laugh. Eventually, walking and standing became harder and harder for Qe. A sweet friend surprised him with a four-wheel rollator walker with a seat. Qe was grateful to the point of tears. It was awesome to see his excitement for something he fought so hard not to need.

Qe loved to cook, and it had become extremely challenging for him to balance while maneuvering around the kitchen. The assistance of the walker allowed him the flexibility to continue cooking. He was so excited and said "Ma, I can roll around the kitchen and still cook while you're at work!" His independence meant everything to him. His happiness and excitement was like striking water in the middle of the driest desert.

There was always this short period of sickness and great fatigue he would go through as a side effect from the radiation. It would hit Qe pretty hard, and I always attempted to brace him for this in whatever way I could. It usually started toward the end of the 15th day of radiation and lasted a little over a week. He would lose his appetite and lose a few more pounds. His mood would change drastically and he stayed in bed almost the entire time.

Once that particular round of radiation and the side effects were over, his walking appeared to become stronger overnight, and he looked great in spite of all he had endured. He was able to walk steadily without the walker. The radiation had shrunk the tumor affecting his walking. We were all happy and beyond hopeful! One day I noticed him getting dressed, and I asked him where he was going. He said that he was taking his girlfriend out on a date because he hadn't been able to do anything for her in a while. My heart melted at his selflessness, and I was overjoyed to see him doing something other than going to another doctor's appointment. I admit that I was a little nervous because he was still a little weak, but moments of normalcy like these were like taking a breath of fresh air.

In the meantime, while I was so focused on a miracle for Qe'Vonte, God was working on a miracle in another area of my family. Xzavier was distant even though he came home periodically. When he did come around, he was high, and this agitated me more than anything. I would fuss at him, which always turned into an argument. It happened over and over, but nothing was changing. After I realized my approach wasn't making things any better, I started going to my room when he came home. I would sit in silence and talk to God about my frustrations. This was my attempt to avoid getting frustrated. I knew in my heart it was no use for me to keep getting upset over his actions and going through the same thing over and over. My heart longed for Xzavier to step up and help me during this crucial time.

Gradually, I changed my habits from fussing to praying. Each time he came home high, I would just go in my room and say a small prayer to God. I expressed everything I would have usually said to Za, but I was telling God all about it. I communicated all of my frustrations about Za each time. After about two weeks of me doing this, Xzavier came to me one day asking me if he could go to church with me. That alone was enough for me to know his heart was changing, because Xzavier had not gone to church with me in a few years—at least not willingly. I started noticing that he was staying around the house a little more too. On the Sunday Xzavier went to church, after the sermon was preached he walked up to the front of the church to give his life to Christ. He said, "I just want to make it back home." This was in direct response to the sermon preached that day which was about heaven being a Christian's home. He also told them he wanted to be baptized. I was overjoyed to see him make the decision to give his life to Christ for himself. This was a miracle.

I came to realize the lesson God wanted me to learn when I became tired of fighting with Za to do what was right, and started taking my frustrations and burden for him directly to the Lord instead of trying to fix things myself. This happened to be the very thing that God was looking for to perform a miracle in Xzavier's life. Za didn't need another lecture from me. He needed Jesus to come into his heart. As I was believing so adamantly for a physical healing for Qe, Za was in just as much need of a spiritual miracle. He needed to make an exchange of his burdens and personal pains with the freedom that is in Christ. Xzavier was so excited about changing his life around. This moment was like one of those unexpected night-blooming flowers from God.

While it appeared that Qe was getting stronger, I knew we weren't safe from the dangers of cancer. I was relieved by his progress, but I told Qe we couldn't relax until the cancer was completely gone. The path to remission always felt tedious. Until then, it was imperative that we stayed focused. I often told Qe that I would always give him my very best. This stemmed from the fact I was a very young parent, then spent most of the journey as a single parent. The road for me had been full of hardships. I never wanted him to feel life had shortchanged him because of my challenges. He also heard me reiterate this during times I was pushing him in school, the workplace, or just life. Now I was saying it because I wanted to see him live a long life with all of God's abundant blessings. I wanted to see him healed. He would just smile big and say, "Yes ma'am, I know Ma."

CHAPTER
ELEVEN

Before Midnight

The long streak of victories throughout Qe'Vonte's battle with cancer caused Qe to become complacent too soon. Even with the best efforts, a life can still be lost to cancer. Cancer doesn't care who or how aware you are; it still hits hard. Maybe my perspective was shaped by the years of being in and out of Birmingham Children's Hospital and the hardships that came along with that journey. Nevertheless, we couldn't afford to let our guard down just because Qe was appearing stronger.

Qe started to be gone more and more. I was uneasy with him being away from home so much, and I let him know I felt like he was moving too fast. I didn't want him to feel smothered, but I noticed he had lost a few more pounds and was still very weak physically. I could understand that he was eager to be out of the house since during almost an entire summer of intense radiation treatments he had spent a lot of time in bed recovering. His desire to return to normalcy once his strength returned was understandable. I wasn't comfortable with Qe taking care of himself because of his frailties, and I've always been meticulous when it came to caring for him. Some of my friends would joke and say that I had "healing hands" because of all the times Qe would bounce back. I am confident this was because God gave me not only the motherly intuition to take care of him, but even more importantly, the gift of intercession and persistent faith to believe that God could cause Qe to overcome.

Two, three, and four days went by that Qe hadn't come home. When he did, I saw that he was moving some of his belongings out. He was moving back with his girlfriend. My heart sunk because I knew this was too big of a move for him. He had lost so much weight, and he wasn't back at one hundred percent strength. I knew he wouldn't listen to me, so I just said, "So you're leaving Mama, huh?" He smiled and assured me he would be ok. He had just gotten to where he could walk without having his walker. I worried about what this would do to his progress in this extreme uphill battle of getting better. In spite of that, my son's will to be a man was strong, and he fought to be free of the limitations placed upon him by this illness. I saw how much he loved his girlfriend. They were even discussing marriage and creating a family. I could only imagine his hope for enjoying a normal life with her.

Thankfully they lived less than five minutes away. Knowing he was that close soothed my heart. I probably called or texted him every day. I would drop food off to him when I could and checked in with him regularly regarding his doctor appointments. For a few weeks, it began to feel as if we had completely returned to our normal routine like when he was independent, working, in college, and checking in to update me and let me know how everything was going.

Xzavier appeared to be battling internally, and I was trying to figure out how to help him. After he had given his life to Christ, he was home more often. Many nights, I heard him having nightmares, and I would have to go and wake him up. Sometimes it would sound like he was in a horrifyingly scary movie. One night about 2 am he cried out, "Mama… Mama!" I was asleep, and it startled me to hear one of my children calling out for me in such a panic. I stumbled out of bed thinking it was Qe calling me. This was shortly before Qe moved out with Fiancée. But before I could reach Qe's room, he said, "Mama, it's not me—it's Za crying like that!" Za was sweating profusely and whimpering like a small boy and murmuring. I woke him while rubbing his head and praying over him. I was so shocked and taken aback that Za was battling in such a way. This episode turned out to be one of many. When I asked Za what his nightmare was about, he said there were dark figures chasing after our family, and he was afraid for us.

Though Za was 21, I rubbed his head as if he was my chubby-cheeked little five-year-old Za, comforting and assuring him we were going to be just fine. He said, "Yes ma'am," and peacefully fell back to sleep. I could only imagine how watching Qe suffer and struggle to survive was affecting him and Kayla. I was doing everything in my power to stay upbeat, strong, encouraging, and hopeful for them, but I myself was having panic attacks at night. Ever since the day the doctor told me Qe had only a few months to live, I would wake up many nights thinking I was having a heart attack, feeling dizzy and with my heart racing. I had never experienced that before. I could tell the entire ordeal was taking a toll on us. Kayla also shared how she too had sleepless nights, but somehow overall she was able to maintain a quiet strength. I saw her gain peace and strength just being by Qe's side and holding on to the hope that he was going to get better.

One night after Qe had moved out, I noticed Za didn't come in. I saw him sitting outside with a friend about 1 am, so it was odd that he wasn't home at six am. Routinely he would stretch out across my couch and sleep in until about noon. Later that day, I received a call with a robotic introduction: "This is Madison County Jail, would you like to receive a call from…" and my heart dropped. The second I heard the recording, I knew it was Xzavier, and the timing couldn't be worse. He told me that he was feeling depressed and couldn't sleep. So he decided to go and get something to help calm him. I knew this meant marijuana. He said he was walking home and he was stopped by the police. When they saw he had drugs on him, they arrested him because he was already out on parole.

As he was talking, I felt numb to what he was saying. I was tired of being angry, tired of saying everything I had already been saying to warn Za of his bad habits and behaviors. I had compassion and empathy for his struggle, but I couldn't approve of his bad decisions. I attempted to bail him out so that he could continue to be there with the family to support Qe, but a hold was put on bailing him out from his parole officer. Though Xzavier had given his life to Jesus Christ, he now had to learn how to allow God to be his only crutch in times of depression or worry instead of drugs.

This was his journey with God, which I believed would eventually be a sure path to freedom for him.

Two weeks later, Qe texted me asking if he could move back home. I was so excited to see his text, I said, "Sure son!" Then he sent another text saying, "I'm sorry I have to keep coming back Ma." Saddened that he felt this way, I assured him that I'd rather him be under my roof than not during such a crisis in his health. I told him I was happy for him to move back and reassured him that he was always welcome. I went to pick him up right after work that day. Kayla and I were both excited about him coming home. Even though he had only been gone for a couple weeks, it felt like forever. As I watched Qe come down the stairs and make his way to my car, I could see that his walking had become impaired again. He plopped down in the passenger seat and said, "What's up, Ma?" accompanied by his famous smile.

Kayla and I helped him get settled back in and comfortable. He was bothered by nerve pain all throughout his body and was not feeling well. He was in bed and rested for several days. One morning when I went in to take him an extra blanket, I noticed his hip bones protruding. I almost gasped because I didn't know he had lost that much weight, but I could tell he was looking at my response. I made no big deal of it and continued to change his covers. I would guess he had lost another seven to ten pounds. You could not tell this by looking at his face, and his clothes covered his frame.

He woke up the following Sunday morning and said "Ma, I can't feel when I have to pee. I think I need to go to the emergency room." We were at a point that Qe was only being offered pain management because the doctors felt there wasn't much else that could be done, but we didn't want to let this go unaddressed. Because he had sporadically experienced this before, we both thought that maybe this was just a temporary thing happening due to the tumors pressing on his nerves. We decided to go if he felt the same after I came home from church. Qe decided to come sit in the front room with Kayla since he had been in the bed for a couple of days.

As he was maneuvering his walker, I could see that he was struggling even harder than he had just a couple of days ago. Little did I know how much he was actually struggling until later. I asked him if he needed help, and he said "I got it, Ma." He inched each foot in front of the other, and when he got to the couch he plopped down with a huge sigh of relief. I prepared breakfast for him and Kayla before I left for church. As I did so many other times, I whispered to Kayla to watch Qe closely because she was my right hand throughout this journey. I kept my phone by my side the entire service, my eyes glancing down at my phone in between my "Amens" and praising God in spite of my circumstances. I finally received a text from Kayla saying Qe wanted to go ahead and go to the emergency room. I left church alarmed because Qe rarely ever wanted to go to the doctor, let alone the emergency room.

When I walked through the door, I could see the despondent look on his face. I told Kayla to gather her things because I knew we could be at the hospital for some time. I went to help Qe stand so I could help him walk to the car, and as I helped him stand his legs gave out completely. I grabbed him with all my strength, and I called out to Kayla for her help. We sat Qe back down on the couch, and I asked if he was ok. I wasn't sure if I had hurt him or not. This came as a huge surprise to me that he couldn't stand at all. I knew he had struggled to get to the living room that morning, but I didn't realize it had gotten this bad so fast.

I knew this was more than likely one of those situations where Qe may not have been communicating his symptoms as he noticed them happening. I found out a few weeks later that walking was more challenging than he initially let on. He told me that he was using his hips to swing one leg in front of the other because he could barely lift his legs. You couldn't tell this by looking at Qe. My mind was racing about how to get him transported to my car. Should I call the ambulance? Could Kayla and I carry him to the car together? I called Boniechia to ask if Kris could help, but he was over 30 minutes away. She reminded me that one of my close friends lived right down the street. Melvin and Toya Poplar are dear friends to our family and Qe'Vonte loved them. I reached out to them, and Melvin came to lift Qe and carry him to my car.

As I pulled into the emergency room garage, I realized that I would need help getting him out of the car. I was in a bit of shock and never had to plan around this type of circumstance. An employee walked up and asked what the emergency was. I told him my son had cancer and wasn't able to walk. So the gentleman went to get a wheelchair. When he returned, he positioned the wheelchair by the passenger door, as if he was waiting for Qe to get out. I had to remind him that Qe could not stand on his legs and we needed help. The man then leaned over and said, "What's wrong with him?" in the worst attempt at a whisper. Besides the extreme irritation with the guys' rudeness, I immediately thought about how often this must happen to people who are disabled, people seeing the disability and treating them as if they can't see or hear. With Kayla's help, I managed to lift Qe into the wheelchair as the guy held the wheelchair still. Qe looked irritated with the whole ordeal. After I got him and Kayla situated in the waiting room, I ran out to park my car.

CHAPTER
TWELVE

GRASPING FOR HOPE

Qe'vonte was admitted to the hospital. The doctors scheduled an MRI to pinpoint what was causing the paralysis and incontinence. His room was on the 7th floor, which I heard a nurse refer to as the cancer patients' floor. Doctors and nurses came in and out evaluating the state of his paralysis. They were astounded that he could still slightly move one of his feet but not his legs. The MRI later revealed that a tumor was pressing on his spinal cord in his lower back.

He still had feeling in his legs as well. They called it partial paralysis, but said it was rare. Grasping for hope, I took this as a sign that Qe would regain mobility. He also had to have a catheter inserted. He would look at me periodically and say, "Good thing I can't feel much below my waist," with a huge smile, and we would both laugh. His humor would come at the perfect time. It gave me the strength I needed during the times I was extremely tired or saddened by what he was going through.

At this point, I was dealing with some frustration. I regretted that he left and moved back out for that short time. I believed that even those few days could have made a tremendous difference in the outcome of his healing. His girlfriend, Fiancée, later shared with me that she would see him struggling more to walk or experiencing more pain. She would suggest to him that he needed to go to the doctor, but he would get frustrated or would say he would go but wouldn't. However, he would faithfully go to physical therapy. I understood more clearly why Qe asked to come home after talking with Fiancée. He knew his health was declining, but he had not shared it with me. I wished he would have, so that I would've been more prepared for what was about to happen.

I came home from church to a paralyzed Qe which seemed so sudden from my viewpoint. I'm sure in his heart, he was probably scared or hoping that it would turn around and get better like it did before…I don't know. But I felt blindsided, and was frustrated, thinking those few weeks he had moved out were weeks I could have been caring for him and helping him heal. It was hard to experience such success in battling cancer in the past, only to watch Qe's condition worsen in the present. I was exhausted, but I didn't have time to focus on my fatigue. All I could think of was how tired Qe must have been considering that his body was taking all the blows and punches. I laid aside frustration to focus on my faith. Besides, I could only imagine that my meager efforts toward contributing to his healing would have made the monumental difference I desired.

Whenever Qe was admitted into the hospital, it was as if I was checking in also. I felt responsible for remembering all the information we were being given about his condition, realizing how easy it is to forget something when you are receiving constant medical updates. One piece of information could change anything, and I had little confidence that Qe would not forget something important. Most importantly, I never wanted Qe to feel like he was alone. I also wanted to cater to his love for food by making sure he had whatever his wavering appetite craved. It wasn't easy to do, especially since I had just advanced to a new position at work about a month prior, and I was trying to not to take too many days off. This promotion was a blessing for our family both financially and medically. My new position as a web analyst enabled me to seek out better care for Qe. Up until this time, we hadn't had medical benefits. Whenever I thought Qe was good and comfortable, I went to work. My routine was to stop by the hospital before work and during my break, and return immediately after. A few days into this routine, as I was on my way to work, I received a call from a nurse saying that he had blood in his urine. I made a u-turn to head to the hospital.

When I arrived, Qe had his cover over his head. He said his stomach hurt. Having a cover over his head was always a sign that he was in excruciating pain or didn't want to be bothered with anyone. As a teen, he wore a hoodie to his outpatient chemotherapy sessions. Covering his head was a way for him to create a place of comfort and escape.

His feet were swollen and felt cold to the touch. When I questioned the nurses and doctors about it they attributed it to poor circulation stemming from lying in bed for so long. I informed family and friends that Qe was back in the hospital, so that prayer warriors could pray. A test was ordered by the doctor to find out why he had blood in his urine. The next day, I went to work. I could barely focus with Qe so heavily on my mind. I left a little early that day to be by Qe's side and find out the results from the test. When I walked in his room, I could smell that he had soiled himself. The room was cold and dark. Qe was balled up in the fetal position under blankets. Wondering how long he had been in this state, I asked Qe with panic in my voice, "Are you okay?! Where is your nurse?! Are you in pain?" He was in extreme pain. He had called out for the nurse but she hadn't responded. Only God knows how long he had been waiting.

I could feel my blood boiling as I raced to the nursing desk in search of his nurse. The nurses at the station could tell I was upset. They located his nurse quickly and had her come to attend to Qe. If you knew my son's personality, you would know that he was such a low maintenance person that by the time he actually mustered up enough strength to ask for help, he had to really be suffering. Being incontinent was not only embarrassing for him, but it was also discouraging beyond words. The thought of his needs being ignored, or him not receiving the care that he needed was both heartbreaking and infuriating.

The nurse finally came in fidgeting around, and I asked her if the results had come back from his urine tests. She hesitantly said that she had not sent it off yet. It was evident at this point that my concerns about the care and attention he was receiving weren't just the product of an anxious mother, but were legitimate and valid. I realize that she may have been loaded down with work or having a bad day, but it's hard to care about that when your child has been in extreme pain all day and lying in his own feces. I regretted going to work that day. It was about 5:30 in the evening, and another day had gone by without us knowing the reason he had blood in his urine. After this I continued to stick close by his side to ensure he was receiving quality care. From that moment I took off work indefinitely. My bosses and coworkers were a godsend. They were understanding and patient, and extended some much-needed grace.

Qe's test results revealed that he had a urinary tract infection. His stomach pains were a result of bladder spasms, which were triggered by the infection. At one point, I saw the nurses become alarmed, and they told me they were calling for the doctor. Qe'Vonte's blood pressure had dropped. I can only remember that the top number was 50 over another number. I was ignorant on the topic of blood pressure. Neither I nor anyone around me had ever had blood pressure issues, so I didn't understand the severity initially. They said they had to transfer him to the ICU to receive a special medication to get his blood pressure back up. I began packing up everything in his room. As I did so, a doctor that we were more familiar with from Clearview Cancer Institute came in to see Qe. It was good to see a familiar face.

She sat down on the side of Qe's bed as she began to speak to us about all the present issues he was facing. She then graciously asked Qe if his heart stopped or any of his organs failed, would he want to be resuscitated. He said no with no hesitation at all, and I burst into tears. The pain seemed to hit me right in the chest, to hear my son say this. I fought to pull myself together. But I also couldn't believe that he had come this far to be on the brink of losing his life under these circumstances. I had never heard of a DNR (Do Not Resuscitate) order before now. Not in a million years could I have ever chosen to not resuscitate Qe. This was a hard reality for me to accept, and it felt like my heart was being crushed even more.

One day, my brother stopped by to see Qe during this time he was in the hospital. I left the room to give them a little privacy. Later on my brother mentioned how Qe shared a hard truth that day. He said, "I wish I could go to sleep and not wake up, so this can be all over with." It took me by surprise that Qe's emotional state had come to this. I was also taken back because he had never come close to sharing anything of this sort to me. However, I did notice he'd become very withdrawn and quiet. I was shocked and deeply saddened by what his emotional and mental state had become. But as I began to reflect, I realized that from our own unique perspectives of this trial, we were attempting to protect each other. Not only was I blinded by my persistent faith, but also by my lack of experience. Eventually, I had to face that my best efforts could not prevent him from slipping into a state of decline both in his health and emotional wellbeing. I felt more and more helpless day by day.

After being transferred to the NICU because the regular ICU was full, they worked hard to get Qe's blood pressure stabilized. We were a couple of doors down from the same place Qe was in when he was initially admitted five months before. This was the time we were first told he had six months. It was as if we circled around the block to end up right back where we started, but it was worse. Qe became even more withdrawn. I didn't know what to do, so I simply sat by his bedside and talked to God as I attempted to fight back the tears. I cried so many quiet tears when he was asleep.

The visiting hour rules were more strict in the NICU, so I stayed until they closed, then returned first thing in the morning when the doors opened. One thing that always made me feel better about leaving him was befriending the nurses. This helped reassure me that Qe would be handled with care and concern and that he would be watched closely. The next day, I would be there when the doors opened.

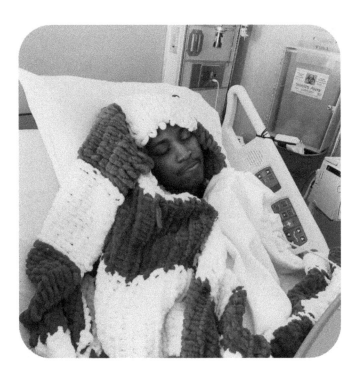

WHAT IS LONG LIFE?

Qe became so withdrawn and quiet. It was as if he was pushing me and Kayla away from him. He had also given me his wallet and phone, which I assumed was because he wanted to make sure I kept up with them until he got out of the hospital. He didn't speak at all about how he was feeling emotionally. I interpreted his quietness and serious demeanor as him being in physical pain or just pure exhaustion from going through it all. He wouldn't eat most of the time. He'd manage to take a couple of bites of food periodically, and this was only because the nurses told him they couldn't give him pain meds if he didn't eat.

Wishing I could just rescue him and take him to a place that cancer didn't exist consumed my thoughts. My favorite movies were about superheroes who were once underdogs who won the battle against all odds. My inner artist imagined picking Qe up and supernaturally swinging him into the literal arms of God. I wanted to be the superhero that could throw him past the clouds and stars right into heaven and into God's embrace. I knew Qe would be safe and permanently rescued from all the evils that were coming against him. Just entertaining the thought gave my aching heart comfort. One day, I stood in the hallway of the hospital sharing this with my dear friend Jemeana, and she cried with me. I thought I sounded foolish but instead, it was as if she could feel my pain and she empathized with me.

One day Qe's physical therapist, Edward Goodman III, and his wife Donna, stopped by to visit us. I met them downstairs in the hospital lobby because Qe wasn't feeling well enough to receive visitors that day. As we sat and began to talk, Donna began to describe things in Qe's behavior that I hadn't yet shared with her, so I was all ears for what she had to say. She asked if he was withdrawn and not wanting to talk or interact as much. She went on to say that she had taken care of several family members before they transitioned from this side of heaven to the next. I could see the compassion and empathy in her eyes when she looked at me and said, "He's ready to go Rosemary. These are all signs that he is letting go of this life." I burst into tears, overwhelmed by the emotional weight of what was becoming our reality.

Although this caught me by surprise, I knew that God was enlightening me because my heart was heavy due to the change in Qe's behavior. I had come to a place that I was so focused on his healing that these words deeply pierced my soul. I quickly realized that maybe our faith was pointed in two different directions. Whereas I was believing for him to live, Qe had reached a point of letting go. I was doing my best to grapple with this and readjusting my approach to the situation with Qe because I respected his stance. I was respectful of the fact that he was the one suffering from this illness, not me. But I knew it wouldn't stop my prayers for what my heart desired. I was convinced that if God healed Qe, his perspective would change.

Robert, Qe's dad, also shared with me a day or so later that Qe asked him to watch after me and his siblings if he didn't make it. Robert went on to share how he felt like Qe was a type of angel because of his love and selflessness as he broke down in tears. I felt so out of sync with Qe's emotional state. I realized that he was purposely shielding me from these thoughts and emotions. But I didn't want to be kept in the dark. Both of us were being so strong for each other that a wall had formed between us. I had to search within myself how to address the topic of death...more specifically, Qe's death. As always, the grace of God enlightened me to at least break the silence on my end. I knew that even in this state, God didn't intend for us to be overtaken by sadness and depression, so I focused on what could bring us joy. My family's love for each other was that joy. I also began focusing on the present moments versus how much time he had left or even the faith aspect of the journey.

I walked in his room that next morning determined to encourage him as I also encouraged myself. I told him that whether God gave him ten days or ten years, every moment God gives us is filled with purpose, so we were going to keep our heads up and be grateful. I kissed his forehead and expressed how much I loved him, and I was determined that every second would at least be approached with thanksgiving and joy. Taking on this mindset gave me a sense of peace. By the grace of God, we were able to maintain our joy in the midst of trauma and grief.

Qe and I had a tough talk in which I was able to share my observations of how he was pulling away. It wasn't hard for me to empathize with him, because I too, was mourning the loss of his independence. I could only imagine the weight of what he was feeling. Regardless, I needed him to understand how this was hurting his sister and me even more. I'm not an end-of-life expert at all, but I chose to believe that this distance between us did not have to be this way. Why couldn't we focus on making the best of every second we had by loving each other and being joyful? This reflected who we were as a family more than anything. If we were coming to the end of Qe's journey on earth, we should make the best of it. This was my faith. I told him that I was fine if he was tired and ready to be with God, even though I truly wasn't. I believed he needed to hear that from me so he wouldn't feel the need to shield me from his truth. I rested in the fact that regardless of how he felt, God held Qe's life and the number of days in His hands. One day, as Qe was staring up at the TV, I saw a few tears fall from his eyes. Nothing had been said, and I didn't want to question his tears. I gently wiped his face and sat back in my seat. Even up until this point I had rarely seen Qe cry, so I knew it was something heavy on his heart. I just sat by his bed in silence and prayed.

After a couple of days in the ICU, Qe's blood pressure regulated and they transferred him back to a normal room. He was still a little quiet, and I allowed him that space. We looked for where we would go from here in regards to him coming home. I was struggling with coming up with a plan because I knew I would need help with caring for Qe now that he was paralyzed. The only option that seemed to provide what we needed was hospice. But, I still rejected the thought of hospice because I associated it with accepting my son was going to die. For this reason I began seeking out other home health options. However, after nurses and doctors spoke to Qe about what he wanted to do, he accepted hospice as the plan of care when he was discharged.

I started crying, which I had fought so hard not to do in front of him throughout this journey. I kept saying, "It just doesn't feel real... This just doesn't feel real." Qe said, "Sometimes things look like the end but it's only the beginning," with a stern stare and serious demeanor. I honestly didn't even know how to take or digest what he said. I wiped my tears and continued on planning to get him home. To give my joy a focal point, I zeroed in on the holidays. It was about a week before Thanksgiving. Thinking about how to make my children happy during this time helped me not to give in to the temptation to be overcome with sadness. In the meantime, Qe was still on antibiotics for the urinary tract infection and blood was still in his urine.

One particular Sunday immediately after church, my pastor, Pastor Emma White, and her daughter Knegleshia came to visit Qe. After everyone greeted him and spoke to each other, Pastor White asked for everyone to step outside the room, so she could speak with Qe alone. Robert, Knegleshia, and I all went downstairs to the store to grab a few snacks. When we arrived back to the room, Pastor was on her way out. She looked at me and Robert and said with tears in her eyes, "You have a rock in there!" Pastor shared a few details of their conversation, but there were a couple of things that hit my heart the most.

Qe told her that he had lived a long life. Hearing this made me speechless. How could my son, a 23-year-old, feel that he's lived a long time? He also expressed that he was tired and ready to go. Qe told her that he had been struggling inside and praying to God asking if his soul was ready to make it to heaven. This helped me to understand Qe's solemn attitude. It bothered him so badly that he could barely sleep the night before. He said that he knew it was God sending her to him because he hadn't told anyone how he felt. He told her that he didn't want to scare me with his concern for his soul's readiness for eternity. Qe also told her that his desire was to leave behind the suffering and go to heaven. But my pastor prayed with him and assured him that his life was in God's hands and that his time here was ultimately God's decision. My pastor also shared how Qe smiled big when we all first left the room. This gave me great joy because it had been a couple of weeks since I had seen Qe smile. Knegleshia also mentioned that when Qe first saw our pastor walk in the room, tears began to fall from his eyes as he looked away from us toward the window.

As his mother, I was so proud to know he was establishing his own position with God. Qe knew how to pray to God for himself, and he had not made himself dependent only on my faith. Qe had gained peace with his righteousness in God, and I embraced this with great joy. I never mentioned my conversation with our pastor to Qe afterward. I was grateful that Qe had peace regarding his soul's salvation.

I had been telling God that He had to grant Qe long life, and that had to happen because that's what He said in His word. It was sort of my attempt to hold God accountable to His word that Qe couldn't die because God promised us a long satisfied life. God was uniquely responding to my prayers by enabling me to see that "long life" was not exactly what I understood it to be. Qe told our pastor that he had lived to see and experience a lot of good things. He knew what it was to be happy and experience great sorrow. He felt contentment from the life he lived. As Paul had found a sense of contentment, Qe did too.

> *Actually, I don't have a sense of needing anything personally. I've learned by now to be quite content whatever my circumstances. I'm just as happy with little as with much, with much as with little. I've found the recipe for being happy whether full or hungry, hands full or hands empty. Whatever I have, wherever I am, I can make it through anything in the One who makes me who I am. —Philippians 4:11-13 (MSG)*

He expressed how the cancer had come back five times, so his life had been spared many times. As I listened to her tell me what he said about how he felt, Qe's viewpoint was like listening to an elderly wise man. The more I reflected, I understood that God was showing me that long life was not an actual reference to the time frame in which we live, but a reference to the quality and level of experiences we encounter. I could no longer use this passage of scripture to suggest that God had not fulfilled a promise to us. To know that Qe felt he'd had an overall good life, gave me such peace. God's promises are not bound to the limitations of time.

CHAPTER
FOURTEEN

GOD IS NOT A LIAR

After Qe had been hospitalized for almost a month, it was finally time for him to come home. I had to reorganize everything in his room for hospice to move in their (hospital) bed and other equipment. On the day of discharge, the paramedic transported Qe home from the hospital. Since we were just a few days away from Thanksgiving, I focused on doing whatever it took to make this a happy time for my children. This also helped me to retain my joy. I was mentally unprepared for what to expect in caring for Qe now. I had no experience taking care of someone paralyzed, but a prior job working at a local nursing facility over ten years before this came in handy for so many upcoming tasks I would be faced with. I was so nervous at what to expect at this stage of caring for him because while he was strong and independent, he had also become frail and vulnerable.

Qe's life felt like it was slipping through my fingers, and it was agonizing to my soul. The times I felt low in spirit I encouraged myself. I often told Qe that I would go down fighting before I gave up on believing he would be healed. Faith permitted me to keep fighting when all the evidence in front of me told me I was crazy for still believing. But frustration with God's timing was brewing in my heart. What was taking God so long to see that I trusted Him—that I believed?! I knew He would heal Qe, if only I believed. The pain of watching Qe suffer, and Kayla bear a burden I didn't believe she deserved, was beginning to feel unbearable. Xzavier was prevented from seeing Qe's physical decline because he was in jail. Some things he didn't have to witness like Kayla and me. Maybe it was God protecting Za from seeing more than what he would have been able to bear. I felt more urgently than ever before that God needed to act and move on Qe's behalf.

I thought if God would just heal Qe, he would desire to live again. I couldn't have faith in God to heal Qe and skip over Qe's will to live. I prayed with a heavy heart, reminding God of His word in Numbers 23:19, that He was not a man that He should lie, nor the son of man, that He should repent. Once, I angrily asked Him, "Are you not a man that you should lie or repent?! Are you a liar God?! Haven't I been faithful?!" I had never felt such anger fueled by desperation before. My reverence for God would only allow me to go so far in my rant. But God did not forget my rant or petition. In desperation, I wanted to provoke God to action by challenging Him with His word. That following Sunday in church, God answered me through the sermon preached. Midway into Pastor White's message, she looked in my direction and said (to the audience), "God said, no I am not a liar." Because I knew I had approached God with an attitude of shaking my fist at him about what His word said regarding healing, I repented. With the fear of the Lord in my heart, I inwardly agreed with the word of God.

Though I chose to believe and trust God, it didn't soothe the unbearable pain I was experiencing. Every second mattered, and we were running out of time. I kept expecting and believing that God was going to perform a great miracle. I knew the strength of God kept me strong, but my heart ached for my children. My fight was just as much for Kayla and Xzavier as Qe. I didn't want them to experience the pain of losing their brother. Many nights my sleep was interrupted by my heart racing so fast that it would wake me up. I'd never had panic attacks before, so I thought I was having a heart attack the first couple of times. I wrestled through the night with the devastation of Qe's decline.

Now that Qe was home, we had a hospice nurse and health aide visiting approximately two to three days a week. His dad and grandmother Lonnie (GG) from Chicago came to help as well. Because I felt the need was so great, the help provided by hospice didn't feel like much help at all. Friends and family also offered to help where they could, but I knew Qe wasn't in the mood for much company. He was grieving the loss of his legs and still processing his present state of incontinence. Because of this, I tried to give him as much privacy as possible to shelter him from potential shame.

Qe and I had a way of maintaining our composure with each other. Our love was all-enduring. We kept our composure in order to be strong for each other. The emotions that lived behind my smile had grown into deep sadness, grief, and exhaustion. Only God knows all of what Qe was facing emotionally as he often lay quietly in his bed. In between hospice staff and visitors, the house was serene. We both embraced the still quietness. It allowed me to gather my thoughts and emotions about what was happening, and I'm sure it did for him too. Our silence had room to exist in this space as well.

In the spirit of hospice, there's a letting go of continuing care that's expected and agreed on. But it went against all my instincts as a mother. It was unnatural for me to let go and not check his temperature or look for ways for him to improve. I did all I could to give him my best, and doing nothing to help him get better was not only difficult for me to do, but also for me to comprehend. In the biggest fight for his life, was I expected to just let him go? I couldn't. My heart could not surrender to that. I believed that God could still turn things around. I only prayed to God about my expectations at this point; I didn't share this with Qe. I knew he was tired and had accepted the fate of dying, and I didn't want to risk upsetting him by bombarding him with my hope. Instead, I showered him with my love and compassion. Whether I brought his meal or bathed him, I made small, positive confessions or compliments to lift his spirits. It was my subtle way of still fighting and believing. I would tell him how handsome he was or how much I admired his strength. I often assured him that God was with him.

Qe still had a catheter, and he had blood in his urine, which indicated he still had a urinary tract infection. The hospice nurse said that the infection might go away with the antibiotics prescribed by the doctor. He was also taking medicine to help prevent bladder spasms. To my surprise, after assisting him with his first bath, I noticed he also had a bedsore on his backside. It turns out he had developed it in the hospital, and the staff failed to make either one of us aware of this. The hospice aide taught me how to take care of and dress the wound. I had become even more upset with the feeling that he hadn't received the best care possible during his hospital stay. The hospice nurse informed me that bedsores were almost impossible to heal from when a person was bedridden. Nevertheless, I was determined not to let that become true for Qe. I made a plan to turn him every two to three hours when he would allow me.

The more that Qe could get out of the bed, the better. I could only imagine how much Qe missed physical therapy. Periodically, when Kayla came in from school, I had her help me lift him into the wheelchair. He had been in bed for weeks. I asked the hospice staff if there was a machine or something that could help me get him out of bed, since I was alone with him most of the time. But they said that the lift was too big for Qe's room. So I continued to get him in and out of bed when I could with the help of another person.

A few days before Thanksgiving, I asked Qe and Kayla what they wanted on the Thanksgiving food menu. Sometimes we chose nontraditional foods such as my homemade Chi-town Italian beef sandwiches. I hoped Qe's love for food would temporarily take his mind off his suffering. Besides, the circumstances were entirely out of our control. We might as well put our efforts into what we *could* control, which was family time and embracing every moment with joy. Qe shared with me the excitement he had for the food plans he and his grandmother GG already had in the works for Thanksgiving. I was all in! My dear friend Sharon also brought us some home-cooked dishes from her mom, which made our dinner complete.

Thanksgiving provided us the opportunity to focus on family and count our blessings. One time Qe said, "Ma, I don't know how you do it. If I only had half the faith you have, I'd be ok." I took this precious opportunity to assure him that we only need a mustard seed of faith to move mountains. I shared with him how meditating on scriptures day and night contributed to my strength and faith. Every morning, Qe began asking me to pop in the CD of Kenneth Hagin's Healing Scriptures gifted to him by our long time family friend, Joyce. I started noticing that Qe was creating a routine of reading and listening to scriptures every morning. This filled my heart with joy. Once, he asked me to rewind the Kenneth Hagin CD several times because he was writing down the scriptures to look up and meditate. Qe said, "Ma, if God could heal him after being bed bound for months, I know God can do it for me." My heart leaped for joy to hear such a faith confession coming from Qe. I saw Qe's demeanor lifting and his smile returning.

But thou, O Lord, art a shield for me; my glory, and the lifter up of mine head. —Ps. 33:3 (KJV)

Qe loved taking care of himself or, as he called it, "beaming." If he saw an outfit he loved, he'd say it was beaming. I suddenly realized he didn't have a mirror in his room, so I went to Family Dollar and bought him one, along with some Old Spice cologne (his favorite scent at the time), and lotion. When I hung the mirror where he could see himself, he said, "Man, I haven't even thought about looking at myself in the mirror since I've been in the hospital." Something as simple as looking at his reflection made him feel better. I would open the window by his bed for fresh air, and he loved listening to the birds in the mornings. It was amazing how these simple things made us more inclined to enjoy and appreciate life's simplicity during this trial.

We also had an inside joke about his hair. After his last radiation treatment, all his hair fell out, but it was a soft curly texture when it grew back. Kayla would say, "You have Mama's hair now!" Before this, he had coarse hair that was perfect when he had a head full of long locs. I'm sure it was the radiation that somehow altered the texture and characteristic of Qe's hair.

Every time someone referred to his hair texture as being similar to mine, it blessed me. One of the biblical views of hair symbolizes physical strength. After all the chemo and previous radiation, Qe's hair never changed until the last treatment—which is when his virtue had also evolved to a sincere place. It was endearing that his hair texture now looked like mine, but it was even more gratifying that we both shared precious like faith.

We were hard-pressed on every side—yet not crushed. Perplexed, but not in despair. Persecuted, but not forsaken, and struck down but not destroyed. My hope resided in the fact that Qe's time was in God's hand.

But we have this treasure in earthen vessels, that the excellence of the power may be of God and not of us. We are hard-pressed on every side, yet not crushed; we are perplexed, but not in despair; persecuted, but not forsaken; struck down, but not destroyed. —2 Corinthians 4:7-8 (NKJV)

CHAPTER
FIFTEEN

STRONG & COURAGEOUS

E arly mornings I'd sing worship songs to God as I prepared Qe's breakfast. Kayla would be just getting up and starting to get ready for school, and the house would be silent except for my singing. Our mornings felt so peaceful. I knew Qe was listening, and I hoped that he found peace and comfort in me reaching toward the presence of God as I did. Kayla's Thanksgiving school break was over, but her Christmas break was just a few weeks away. We managed to get through Thanksgiving by God's grace without any further complications in Qe's health and with a joyful spirit.

Now that we were somewhat into our new routine, I had to figure out how to go back to work while still taking care of Qe. I had recently taken a four-week leave of absence during his previous hospital stay. I adjusted my schedule to get up an extra hour or so earlier to assist him with bathing and meal prep. I'd take Kayla to school and arrive at work by 9 am. Thank God for coffee because it helped me get through my rigorous mornings. While at work, I texted Qe frequently to check on him. I was comforted by the fact that I was just a few minutes away from home and had the flexibility to leave when needed. At lunchtime, I would have Qe text me his food order, and I would go pick it up and take it to him, then return to work.

I quickly embraced the opportunity to start preparing for Christmas. Our newly-established routine became our new normal and helped us cope. There were days I could tell that Qe was bored, so I attempted to come up with something creative or suggest something I thought he'd love to do. Sometimes he went along with what I had suggested, but most of the time he would respond, "I'm straight Ma—could you pass me the controller (to the PS4)?" This made me chuckle. Many times he wanted to sit in complete silence. Oftentimes we would simply smile at each other, and I'd leave him be until my next peek into his room to check on him. Qe was undemanding and easy to please. It was only hard to know when he was in need or wanted something because he usually never asked. Qe was a fan of street gang and mobster type of movies and series. His watchlist this particular season was Peaky Blinders, Queen of the South, and El Chapo, but he was also a lover of his favorite cartoons such as Crowder, Uncle Grandpa, The Boondocks, and Teen Titans.

One Sunday after church, Pastor White, Elaine, and Jemeana came by to sit and talk with Qe. His room filled with explosive laughter as he and Jemeana played a couple of card games. Their joy shifted the atmosphere of my house. Everything was solemn and quiet before their visit. Their laughter was contagious and spread through everyone in the house. I had two Christmas trees that my friend Jodi blessed our family with, and they were still in the box. Elaine was known for her gift for decor and fashionable style, so when she saw the small Christmas tree that was meant for Qe's room, she immediately began to decorate. I was happy to receive her assistance. The tree for Qe gave his room a touch of the Christmas spirit.

Qe expressed his gratitude often. I would respond to his thank you with a smile and a simple nod. Receiving a "thank you" for something that was natural almost felt undeserved, yet I knew his expression of appreciation was necessary for us both. I would tell him there was no other place in the world I'd rather be than by his side. I was determined to see that he would get better and survive. One time, as Qe appeared to be confused about something, he said, "Ma, I feel like your life is consumed with taking care of me." He went on to express how he wanted me to invest more time in myself. As I looked at him in that bed fighting for his life, I thought how sweet and selfless he was to be so concerned for me.

I explained that I did not view our journey that way. He wasn't being a burden or stopping me from doing more for myself at all. Being his mom and all the responsibilities that came with it were my greatest joy and delight. I assured him this was only a temporary trial and pit stop in our lives that would not last forever. I told him we'd be just fine because God would take care of me. He smiled and agreed. But since I saw how important this was for him to see me invest a little time into myself, I did attempt to do so, taking the opportunity to participate in an upcoming company Christmas party.

This Christmas party was special but a little hard to go to because the year prior Qe was my plus one. At first, I was saddened that our current situation wouldn't allow me to take him with me even though I thought of many ways that I could make it possible. Besides, I knew that Qe didn't want to go in his current condition. He didn't want attention being brought to his paralysis or how much weight he had lost. I even asked to make sure he didn't want to attend the party with me, and he said that he just wanted me to have fun as he gave me the brightest smile. I could only hope that deep down the memories of the previous year's party weren't sad to him because of this year's challenging circumstances. To help lessen any possible sadness, I used a couple of things to create excitement about me going to the party. First, I asked Qe's advice on what to wear because he was big on clothes and style. I also told him I was going to win us an LG TV. LG Electronics (my employer) was known for giving out TVs as raffle gifts during the Christmas party. Qe was excited and would often respond, "Fa sho, Ma!" We loved watching movies and series together, especially during this time he was on hospice. I talked about winning the largest TV just to heighten our excitement. It wasn't a need, but a bigger, brand-new TV would've definitely been the highlight of our movie nights and family time.

I made the conscious daily decision to be strong and courageous for my family because on the inside, I was battling my own fears. It was a matter of life and death whether I chose to be brave and continue to walk by faith. I had to resist giving into the fear of passing by his room and finding out he'd passed away quietly in his sleep. My mind would reflect on how low his blood pressure had dropped at the hospital and the doctor describing to me how his organs could begin to shut down if his blood pressure was too low for too long. Since he was on hospice, I had no way of monitoring this. When I asked the hospice nurse if we could make sure his blood pressure wasn't too low, she explained why we would no longer attempt to monitor because it fell under proceeding with care. I didn't care how they looked at things; I was still believing Qe could come out of this, so I figured out ways to deal with the subject of his blood pressure. I took it upon myself to learn a few things about maintaining a good blood flow. His dad and I got him some leg compression socks and lower leg compression devices. I also assigned Kayla to help me exercise his lower extremities, and she made it fun. I called her his physical therapist. I checked on him throughout the night to ease my anxiety. Kayla always talked about what a light sleeper I was, but now it had become lighter. Ultimately, no matter my efforts, I had to trust God that He would keep Qe's blood pressure stable.

From a very young age, Kayla was naturally inclined to care for those in physical need. When she was in the fifth grade, Kayla was assigned to assist children with Down's syndrome in her school, which she thoroughly enjoyed. The teachers recognized her gift and were highly impressed with her at a young age. When she was only eleven years old, she helped my mom distribute her diabetes shot medicine along with other minor needs. I knew she would love to take on the responsibility of helping Qe with leg and foot exercises. This also helped me greatly, considering all the other daily tasks involved in his care. Qe mentioned how he enjoyed those times of exercising his legs because of his inability to move them himself. From his hips down he couldn't move, except for a little movement in one of his feet where he could still wiggle his toes. He had approximately fifty percent of sensation and feeling (which was mainly in his calves and feet area). Everywhere else below the waist he couldn't feel anything. When it was my turn to exercise his legs, he loved for me to pop his toes. Quirky, I know, but I loved to do it because it was one more thing that made him happy.

Before Qe's paralysis, he had the most bubbly way of entering a room. He would bounce into the room with his galactic smile and tall lanky legs and say, "Yo yo yo—what's up Ma?!" Now it had become rare to hear him say this because he had been bedridden in the house for almost two months. So when I'd return from running errands, I would mimic his "Yo yo yooo," so he would know right off the bat that it was me coming in the house (since he was unable to get out of the bed). Remember, we didn't live in the best neighborhood, so this was a quick way to ease his mind about who was entering. I'm sure he felt even more vulnerable because of his paralysis. So the routine upon me entering the house became me saying "Yo yo yooo" and he'd respond, "Yoooo!" It was just another one of our precious things unique to us.

Like so many others that had crossed our path throughout this journey, the hospice staff showered us with compliments regarding our family's faith, character, and strength. The Lord had allowed this trial to be a testament to God's power in our lives. During this season, because it felt like our lives were on display before so many people, I often connected with the moment Jesus stood outside Lazarus's tomb right before He called him forth from the grave.

Jesus said to her, "Did I not say to you that if you would believe you would see the glory of God?" Then they took away the stone from the place where the dead man was lying. And Jesus lifted up His eyes and said, "Father, I thank You that You have heard Me. And I know that You always hear Me, but because of the people who are standing by I said this, that they may believe that You sent Me." Now when He had said these things, He cried with a loud voice, "Lazarus, come forth!" And he who had died came out bound hand and foot with grave clothes, and his face was wrapped with a cloth. Jesus said to them, "Loose him, and let him go." John 11:40-44 (NKJV).

Jesus stood outside Lazarus's tomb with a crowd as He was about to raise Lazarus from the dead. This crowd was about to witness a miracle, which would bring much glory to God. For all of the people God was allowing to witness Qe's tribulation and my turmoil, I believed He was allowing our crowd to form as He was setting the stage for Qe's miracle as well, just like He did for Lazarus. This is what I believed and held firmly in my heart.

With Christmas right around the corner, I thought some Christmas photos would be fun. I needed someone who could make a house call for our photoshoot since Qe was bedridden. The perfect person was my dear friend Toya. Her amazing creativity would help us make this precious Christmas shoot happen. She was the perfect solution for our unique circumstances, and she captured moments that will forever be in our family's keepsakes. I also mailed these to Madison County Jail so that Xzavier could enjoy these precious memories of his family. Despite our family's battle, God was our Jehovah-Nissi, which means He was our banner, and these photos captured the joy and love we felt for one another.

CHAPTER
SIXTEEN

FAITH DON'T FAIL
ME NOW

Christmas was an enjoyable time for us. It was filled with heartfelt gifts, surprises, and unconditional love. One of Qe's gifts was a Dell laptop. I was especially happy about this gift because my hopes were that it could help Qe start the blog he had talked about developing, begin writing his book, or get inspired to create music again. He had always talked about using his gift for music to become a music producer. During this time, his little cousin Christan was developing his production skills and had become excellent in his craft. I would bring one of Chris' beats for Qe to listen to. Qe would look amazed and say how proud he was of his little cousin's work. One day, Qe shared how listening to Chris' music was the inspiration he needed to start creating music again. I hadn't seen Qe excited about any of his passions in life in months, so my heart was overjoyed. In the meantime, Qe was still meditating on Healing Scriptures and listening to Kenneth Hagin's *God's Medicine*.

My joy rested in seeing my children happy and comfortable. Yet I was also beginning to feel the weight of responsibility becoming heavier by the moment. The short drives I once took to clear my mind or catch my breath seemed to not be enough anymore. The few visits a week provided by hospice personnel were not enough for the daily demands. Considering that my belief was that Qe would live beyond this, I started considering other home care options. Maybe they could provide more frequent visits and help Qe with physical therapy that could help strengthen him. I was pressed and tired, but I thought it best to keep to myself. The burden I had been carrying in this fight for months began to weigh more on me emotionally and physically. Anything that gave me hope fueled my strength and that's what I held firmly to. When I saw Qe's, Za's, and Kayla's joy, it gave me the strength to keep pushing, assuring myself that God would divinely heal Qe soon.

Sometimes I felt like Qe and I were in a battle scene like those I'd seen in war movies, where there were two soldiers on a battlefield. One brave soldier would attempt to carry a badly wounded comrade out of harm's way, while the battle raged around them. The stronger soldier would carry the injured soldier on one side while still shooting with the other hand and dodging bullets from the enemy. To imagine the full amount of Qe's weariness along with the blows he had taken made me desire as well as attempt to carry him to safety. No matter what it cost me, my goal was to carry him to victory. Whatever he lacked, my determination was to believe it down from heaven. I didn't consider myself to have much, but I knew faith was my secret weapon.

I know this may be a bit dramatic of a scenario to compare our situation to, but this is how I felt. Losing this battle was not an option. No matter how worn out I may have been, I couldn't afford to stop. I had to keep fighting for Qe until his health was restored. I could strongly relate to the exhaustion, weariness, or pain a soldier would feel after a long heated battle. Yet I was looking forward to winning the victory. I could only imagine how much more intense Qe's experience was. On days that I felt like I had run out of strength, I imagined myself being the stronger soldier carrying Qe out of harm's way. Envisioning this reinforced my will to not give up. Within my heart, I believed that God wouldn't put more on us than we could bear. We were at a crossroads and in need of a miracle. Doctors suggested hospice for Qe in June 2019, and it was now the beginning of another year, January 2020. It had been a long brutal fight up until this point. Qe had been in hospice care for approximately eight weeks.

One morning, Qe and I were laughing and talking, and he said, "Ma, I wouldn't mind fighting if there is something out there that could help me." Those words were like rain in a desert. I had respected his wishes by bringing in hospice care and only prayed that his heart would desire to live again. The spark of desire to live in Qe's eyes made me feel an inexpressible hope that he would live past the doctor's grim projection. I smiled and told him that I would gladly look into it and see what I could find, knowing I'd already been thinking of something in the back of my mind. At one time, there was a discussion between us and the doctors about going to Virginia, New York, or Texas for Qe to receive trial treatments available for neuroblastoma cancer patients.

The program in Virginia was very promising and hopeful until Qe's walking became severely impaired. When the doctor in Virginia heard about it, he called and retracted Qe's invitation. He was concerned that Qe could become completely paralyzed under their care during what would have been a five-week stay. The facility in New York was not only rude and unprofessional, but they seemed to have never made any real attempts to get back with us. But, we never got the opportunity to pursue options available in Texas. No matter the doctor's report, I figured since God created science, Qe could still beat the odds. When you're walking by faith and not by sight, you are going against the grain. But now was a time that regardless of how crazy it appeared, I needed someone to help us. If the smallest window of opportunity would open for Qe to be helped, it would fuel our hope. At this point, I didn't know if I was operating in faith or hope. But since the word of God says, "These three remain, faith, hope, and love..." I felt that maybe if my faith was limping, my hope provided a crutch for my faith to lean on as it carried us to the next stage of this fight.

Earlier in 2019, I had just become acquainted with a cousin on my mom's side of the family that lived in Houston, TX. We hadn't had much conversation prior to a time where she was visiting my mom, but I thought I could reach out to her to see if she had heard of the hospital the trial was at and could give me any insight. Landress began telling me about a hospital called MD Anderson. I had never heard of this hospital before, so I immediately looked it up online. I was impressed with the reviews, discovering it was a world-renowned facility known for providing top-notch treatments for cancer. I immediately submitted a request for an appointment online and to get things moving, I called our local nurse at the cancer center to request a referral. By the time MD Anderson requested it, I wanted to have it ready to provide to them. We had no time to waste.

In order for our referral request to appear somewhat logical, I told the nurse that we were going to visit family in Houston, TX and while we were there we wanted to stop by MD Anderson for their doctors to look at Qe. In actuality, it was the complete opposite. Our main objective was to see their doctors, and then visit my cousin. I intentionally wanted it to sound like it was coincidental to our already made out plans, because by now I felt like I would look completely crazy (to the medical world) to still be attempting to fight for Qe's survival. The cancer center nurse gladly assisted us and got the referral we needed. She had been so resourceful and extremely kind throughout the entire process, and was one of Qe's cheerleaders. She even cried on the phone with me when Qe first became paralyzed. The next hurdle was to get MD Anderson to accept him for any treatments they may have had available. I dreaded they would call and tell me the same thing we had heard so many times before, "Sorry, there's nothing we can do for him." So we prayed for favor.

After conducting business over the phone for Qe, I would go and talk to Qe about his affairs afterwards. He was only in the next room which sometimes I forgot about. Often midway into me sharing, Qe would say, "I know Ma; I was ear hustling." I would respond, "Oh, ok" and laugh. After he told me this a few times, I then started asking him before relaying the conversation, "Were you ear hustling, son?" and he would say "Yes ma'am" and we'd both chuckle. When I told Qe we were waiting to hear back from MD Anderson, he was so excited. A representative called me to confirm Qe's health insurance and retrieve permission to obtain his medical records for their doctors to review. Every detail or update I received, I shared with Qe, and he would smile from ear to ear. The representative told me they would contact me after everything had been reviewed to let us know whether they felt they had some form of treatment for Qe. The next couple of days I was so anxious to hear back from them.

Being able to bring Qe to MD Anderson felt like our very last hope, and I clung to it with unbelievable intensity. There weren't many trials available for neuroblastoma in the US. Desperate did not come even close to describing how I felt. Though Qe ideally set the goal for eating whole organic foods as his medicine, at this stage the cancer had advanced too much to not seek medical treatments. We prayed and sought the Lord for direction.

When the representative finally called us back, he expressed some concerns the doctor had and that he was leaning towards feeling like they would not be able to help us. He suggested that the doctor could give me a call if I had concerns or questions. I told him to please have the doctor call me. I was driving when the representative from MD Anderson called me. After we hung up, as I pulled into the Waffle House parking lot, I desperately prayed and asked God to help me and give me wisdom and favor. The doctor called me back immediately. He was a very kind-spirited man, Dr. Harrison. He began to share some of his concerns about why he felt it was a risk to bring Qe'vonte to Texas from Huntsville. But for every concern he addressed, I had a solution or answer.

One major concern was how long Qe would need to stay in the hospital, something that couldn't be foreseen. He didn't want me to become stranded there without finances (assuming I would be taking off work to be there with Qe). I explained that I was a web content developer. And since I had been permitted to work from home, there wouldn't be any financial strain. All of his concerns were logical and things that I didn't mind addressing to show him how ready and willing we were to come.

I felt as if I was pleading a case on Qe's behalf. I attempted to give this doctor the best condensed version of Qe's entire 15-year journey with cancer I could, along with describing how amazing he was and how he was worth any effort of treatments available.

Most importantly, I expressed to Dr. Harrison how I understood the odds of Qe being saved beyond this stage, so he wouldn't think I was in denial or delusional. I didn't want to be written off as a crazy lady that can't see what's in front of her. I told him that I was very aware and just wanted to fight because he had beaten the odds so many times before. It was my best way of communicating my faith on a level I thought they'd respect. Qe's miraculous remissions over the years could not be denied by anyone in the medical field. Everyone we came in contact with in the medical field (especially toward the latter end of the journey) always acknowledged that Qe surviving neuroblastoma for a 15-year journey was pretty amazing. I would tell them—that's God.

By the end of the conversation, the doctor told me that Qe sounded like a pretty amazing guy. He went on to say that he meets with a team of doctors on Tuesdays regarding all of their patients, and he would talk to them about Qe'Vonte. I must have thanked him a hundred times. I was just happy that he didn't completely shut the door in our face. Qe, Za, and Kayla were excited to hear the news that we were one step closer.

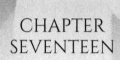

CHAPTER
SEVENTEEN

WHETHER WE STAY
OR GO

As we awaited an answer from the MD Anderson doctors, my need and desperation to get out of the mundane routine we were in felt heavier by the moment. Initially, after coming home from a month's stay in the hospital, we embraced the comfort of our home and our love for each other. It was also a time that we regained strength after experiencing the blow of Qe's paralysis. After eight weeks of him being in hospice care, I began to feel like maybe we needed to get up and go to our miracle. I stood discreetly in my faith to respect Qe's wishes while in my own agony and grief. But now with the hope of taking Qe to MD Anderson, relief was given to my mental and emotional pain. Despite the love and support of our friends and family, we still experienced a measure of isolation and loneliness. We talked about these feelings at times, so some extra mental and emotional support from fresh eyes was more than welcomed. Yet there existed an anxiety within me about whether their analysis would lead us down another dead end of saying there was nothing they could do. I chose to resist these thoughts and believe that God had a plan in which they could help us.

A renewed hope was fueled by the idea of going to MD Anderson. That's all we could talk about throughout the weekend as we anticipated hearing back from the doctor and his team that following Tuesday. During this time, I felt like the four lepers as they conversed with each other in the moment they faced possible death in 2 Kings Chapter 7. The first thing they asked one another was, "Should we sit here until we die?" The sitting and waiting was becoming tiresome and unbearable for several reasons. But the main reason was because with each passing day, we knew Qe was getting closer and closer to death. And I didn't feel that everything possible was done to save him. Many days I thought God permitted more pain than I could bear.

In Kings the Bible says that it happened that four lepers were sitting just outside the city gate. They said to one another,

> *"What are we doing sitting here at death's door? If we enter the famine-struck city we'll die; if we stay here we'll die. So let's take our chances in the camp of Aram and throw ourselves on their mercy. If they receive us we'll live, if they kill us we'll die. We've got nothing to lose."*
> —*2 Kings 7:3-4 (MSG)*

Just as the leprous men counted the cost of staying or leaving their positions in efforts to preserve their lives, I was counting the cost on behalf of Qe. I knew if we stayed, Qe would most likely not survive. At least there was a greater chance of him surviving by going to MD Anderson than by continuing in hospice care. But if there was to be any hope, we needed to leave. As Qe and I weighed our options, we both agreed that at least if we did go to Texas, we would have done all that we knew possible. In addition, the thoughts of the fun we might have gave us immense joy. We talked about all the food we would eat in Houston and this really put a big smile on Qe's face. This trip gave us something to look forward to.

Qe's excitement for the possibility that they could help him was extremely uplifting. But Qe and I agreed that we wanted God to open the door only if it was His divine will. We did not want to hinder God's plan with anything of our own efforts. When the representative did call us back, it was to inform us that the doctors were willing to see Qe'Vonte. I was so excited to run and share the news with Qe! He asked how soon we wanted to come, and I told him I could get him there as soon as they could schedule it. So, we were scheduled that following week for Tuesday, January 14, 2020. I was instructed to take him to their clinic and afterwards he would be admitted from there. The latest time they could schedule him was 2pm in order to catch the team of doctors seeing him before they left for the day.

We were looking at approximately an 11-hour drive, which meant we would have to leave around 1 am to get there on time. I knew this was not a good time for me to drive. I'm more of a get up and start the drive at 3 or 4 am type of chick. If I started driving at 1 am, I would fight sleep horribly between the 3–5 o'clock hours, which I didn't want to do with it being just me and Qe on the road. This meant that I would need to come a day early. I asked the young man if we could come a day ahead and Qe be admitted in.

They said they didn't really set things up like that, but I was free to go straight to the emergency room and from there he would more than likely be admitted in. The plan felt a little shaky for a second, but all I needed was the door to be open. I was determined to make it work. So Qe and I planned to leave the day before at 3 am. To say I was overjoyed was an understatement.

Qe, said "Ma, I need to get a haircut. Do you think auntie Boniechia wouldn't mind cuttin' me up?" I told him that I knew she wouldn't mind at all. Qe said, "Ma, I don't want them to think I'm some scrub and don't care about myself. I want to look presentable." Qe wanted them to have faith that he was worth fighting for. His hair had only grown out just a little since his last haircut. I responded with a smile, inwardly amazed at his point of view. He was the smartest, handsomest, most unique, charming, and ambitious guy I knew, and he didn't need a haircut for anyone to see that. All the same, my heart was glad to oblige him with his humble request. It also amazed me, because in all of our hospital/doctor appointments over the years, I've never seen him want to look "presentable" (in this way) to go see a doctor. Not that he didn't care about his appearance before, but I could understand how this moment was different.

The closer the day came to leave, anxiety began to build inside me. I never showed it because I couldn't afford to. My only option was to be strong. Because I was leaving without knowing how long we would be gone, the trip would just be the two of us. Kayla had to stay behind to keep up with her schoolwork. She stayed with a dear friend of mine whose daughter is one of her best friends, so that would be a fun distraction for her. I loved driving and taking road trips, so I had no worries about making the drive. My anxiety stemmed from the awareness that I needed to get there with as few stops as possible because of Qe's limited stamina for sitting upright and my inability to lift or move him. I knew once I arrived, everything would be fine because I would have the help of hospital staff with Qe, and I could adapt to whatever I needed to for myself. In my slang expression, "I would thug it out," which meant that if I had to sleep on the floor, I would. It didn't matter.

Family and friends were excited about our trip to MD Anderson. I saw people's eyes light up as they shared their excitement and hope for Qe's recovery. Some people were amazed that we were taking our fight all the way to Texas. Some shared how they viewed my attempts to be of great strength and resilience, but I always thought to myself, *wouldn't they do the same thing for their child or loved one? Isn't this what people do when fighting for a life so dear to them?* I never saw it as remarkable as some may have viewed it to be. What people complimented and credited as strength only felt like my duty as a mother to give my son the best opportunity at a good life. But their positive words were encouraging. Beyond the excitement, my anxiety wrestled with what existed in the unknown.

Since the cancer had spread to his brain and spine, Qe had been experiencing anxiety that he periodically took medicine for. I was so intent on focusing on Qe's welfare that I didn't notice my own anxieties until frequent heart palpitations woke me at night. Because I kept assuring Qe I had everything under control when it came to handling his affairs and planning our trip to Texas, I was gradually adding more weight to the pressure I was already under.

I'd rather bear it all than to put anything else on Qe. I knew if God was with me, He would sustain me. My heart wanted God to see my faith and know that I believed in His ability above all we faced. Going to Texas was unfamiliar territory, and I could only hope for the best in uncertainty and be comforted by the fact that God was with us.

The evening before we were to leave, we laughed and talked. Kayla was packing her things to go to her best friend's house. Since his dad had to work, I called Melvin and my brother Lorenzo to arrange for them to come by at 3 am to carry Qe to my car. When Kayla's ride arrived, she went into Qe's room to say her farewell. As I was passing by the room, I saw them giving each other the biggest hug I had ever seen them give one another as they cried. I continued with what I was doing in order to give them the space they needed, and I heard them saying how much they loved each other. It was a moment that would make any mother overjoyed and overwhelmed. It made me more determined to disregard any fears and fight for them. I shed a tear that I quickly wiped away before either of them could see it. I could feel they were saying goodbye as if they didn't know whether it was temporary or permanent. It took my breath away to witness this type of exchange between my children. As Kayla hugged me, I assured her that everything was going to be ok, and that I would update her about every single thing when we got there.

As I was helping Qe pack up some things, I noticed he seemed a little solemn. When I asked him what was wrong, he said that he had a headache. I gave him some medicine and made attempts to help him feel more comfortable. He had begun having periodic headaches in the past couple of weeks, and we both were hesitant to say what we thought was causing it. I knew both of us were wondering the same thing: maybe it was another tumor or growth. Since the tumors had been on his brain and spine, the smallest change usually meant something big. I also started noticing his hands often quivered. This was another red flag. I had to pray against my worst fears and believe God.

After what felt like a nap, I woke up at 2 am to finish loading the car. After I assisted Qe in getting dressed, Lorenzo carried him to my car. As I was loading up a few more bags, Melvin and Qe talked. After the last item was loaded, we said our see-you-laters. Qe and I prayed for traveling grace and we were off.

CHAPTER
EIGHTEEN

WELCOME TO THE MOUNTAINS

W e talked, laughed, and listened to music on our long drive. I wanted to find songs that I thought Qe would like that were already on my playlist. I knew Qe, Za, and Kayla had their own musical preferences, and I didn't want the majority of the 11-hour ride to be just the music I enjoyed. Even when I insisted Qe play some of the songs off his playlist, he would always say, "I'm good Ma. I'm listening to what you're listening to." Qe rarely gave any indication whether he liked what I was playing or not, and I doubt if he knew how hard I was trying to read him to know. Qe and I shared a common ground for music that consisted of more than just liking the same songs. Our love was for the craft of creating music, because he loved to play by ear and produce instrumentals, and I loved being a songwriter. I would find out from some of his friends that he bragged about his mom being a rapper, so I knew he admired my craft. As I scrolled through my playlist, I decided to play a song by Tobe Nwigwe. A minute or so into the song, Qe said, "Ma, who is that? What's the name of that song? That's nice!" I felt like I had struck gold to find music that we both could rock to. So I began to play other songs by Tobe along with some other gospel lyricists as we continued our venture.

Approximately seven hours into the drive, we ran into a storm that produced some very heavy rains. The more I drove, the heavier the rain fell. Visibility became tremendously limited. My driving speed decreased all the way down to about 10–15 miles an hour. For a moment it got so bad that I pulled over and stopped under a very small overpass. I sat there for no more than five minutes before I decided to keep pushing even if I had to drive five miles an hour. It was late in the afternoon, and all I could remember thinking was we're almost there…we're almost there. I was tired and I knew we still had much ahead of us in the day. Qe said, "Ma, I know you can't see, because I can't see the road." I chuckled and said, "Yeah, I can't see that far ahead, but we're going to keep moving slowly." I could tell he was a little nervous. I was definitely more nervous than I was willing to show because I didn't like driving through a storm this heavy in unfamiliar territory. All I knew is that we were somewhere in Texas. I didn't want to prolong our arrival one minute longer.

We were both relieved once we made it into Houston. The rain had lifted a bit, so visibility on the roads was much better. I maneuvered between the large medical facilities and buildings clustered together as I continued to follow the GPS to MD Anderson's emergency room. Once we arrived, I parked right in front of the door to run in and ask for help in lifting Qe. As my eyes roamed across the room, I noticed there was no place to sit because of the crowd. People were coughing and many looked miserable, presumably because they didn't feel well. I was concerned about Qe's immune system and hoped we wouldn't have to sit long before seeing a doctor. As I approached the front desk, I was asked all the questions needed to get him checked in. When they asked where we had driven from, they seemed surprised when I answered Alabama. After completing check in, I asked if someone could help me lift him into his wheelchair, and they immediately called for assistance. Shortly after getting back to my car, two guys came to lift him.

Qe said he was in pain from sitting up so long during the ride. He had not sat up that long in over eight weeks. So his endurance had decreased a great deal. After Qe was comfortably positioned in the emergency room, I ran back out to move my car into the parking garage. I used mental markers to remember where I had parked because the garage was so large. I was watching my surroundings with a great deal of heightened awareness as I walked to find my way back to Qe. There was no place to sit due to the crowding, so I stood by him closely. Even if a seat opened up, I wouldn't move unless there was room for me to position Qe by my side. I gave Qe a banana to eat so that he could take some pain medicine. Minutes felt like hours because Qe's discomfort made me very uneasy. I went up to the front desk several times to ask how long it would be before they'd call his name. I also explained how we had set up an appointment with Dr. Harrison, hoping this would move things along a little faster. They'd answer, "It shouldn't be that long ma'am; someone will be calling him back shortly." Of course, I felt like they were giving me a good enough answer just to get me away from their desk. So I began to pray with urgency.

Looking at the condition of the emergency room made me question bringing him all the way from Alabama. I hoped this was not going to be a worse experience, not after everything we'd endured. After about an hour, they called him back to get vitals, and a very nice lady came to tell me that she had entered Qe in the system to be expedited, and that he would be admitted in and go on to another floor shortly. She spoke softly as if she didn't want anyone else to hear and smiled at me as if she was letting me in on a secret. Whoever she was, I was forever grateful for her because I didn't see her at the front desk initially. I assumed that there was a shift change. Whatever the case, I thanked God for her. Shortly after this, we were escorted to another floor. The atmosphere was much improved. They got Qe into a bed, and he was now able to rest from the long ride. I could exhale…at least for a moment.

Nurses and doctors began to flood the room with questions. It took them a moment to grasp all the details of Qe's condition. His nurse let me know they were in the middle of a shift change. Most questions were asked twice, once by the outgoing nurses and again by the incoming staff as if to confirm what info was passed to them. Once, a nurse even asked if they were understanding correctly that he was paralyzed. It was hard to see the debilitating condition of his health just by looking at Qe. He was clean cut and dashingly handsome. It wasn't until you pulled the covers back that you could see he had almost become skin and bones. Qe rested as I continued to answer all the questions nurses and doctors needed to ask. After a couple of hours passed, I noticed his catheter bag needed to be emptied, so I asked the nurse if she could give me a container to empty it. After it was brought to her attention, she said they would get that taken care of for me. He still had blood in his urine after being on antibiotics for over two months. Qe and I hoped that the doctors here could give us better options for clearing up this UTI.

The first doctor we were greeted by was Dr. Sheila. She was very kind, knowledgeable, and compassionate. After being around doctors for 15 years, you learn to distinguish between doctors who genuinely care and doctors who are simply checking boxes. After answering a series of questions, she immediately started putting in orders for medicines that were different than what he was already taking. Our conversation led us to assume these were better than what he'd been previously prescribed. We were optimistic that it would help relieve some of Qe's suffering. With the most welcoming smile, she looked at Qe and said, "We're going to get you into a room right away." Dr. Sheila addressed the issue of the catheter, and she assured us the UTI was something that could definitely be cleared up. We had heard for weeks that the antibiotic prescribed to him was the only option, but it wasn't helping. Qe and I would discuss how it just didn't make sense because UTIs were so common and supposedly easy to cure. We didn't want the bladder spasms that resulted in excruciating stomach pains to resurface. Her kindness and expertise brought me even more relief. After she left the room, it was just a short amount of time before the staff came to escort us to Qe's new room.

When we exited the elevator onto the ninth floor, it was instantly apparent how remarkable MD Anderson was. We couldn't have foreseen how awesome our experience would be. As we approached his assigned room, we passed by the help desk that was right outside his room. We were greeted with the biggest smiles and extreme kindness. What I had heard Qe'Vonte's entire life regarding his smile and pleasant demeanor was being echoed by the hospital staff in Texas. Qe was showered with compliments about his smile. I stood by as they maneuvered his bed into the room and transferred him into another bed. When I first walked in, I saw "Welcome to the Mountains" written on the white board. After putting my bags down and getting settled in, I couldn't help but reflect on the weight of those words. I stared at it for a time as nurses helped Qe get acclimated, and I reflected on the spiritual representation for me and Qe.

Everything about MD Anderson was like no other previous medical facility experience we had encountered. It was nothing short of excellent. The first 24 hours we were overwhelmed in the best way. I found myself with a migraine and exhausted beyond words. I was in fighting mode because I knew I would have to address the severity and advancement of the cancer. I was prepared to let them know that my hope wasn't rooted in denial. Qe and I would look at each other and smile as we quickly became aware that they had a specialist for everything.

We had visitors nonstop for at least the first 48 hours. One of the first issues they addressed was Qe's bedsores. The primary one on his backside, I had been trying to heal myself. They also pointed out small tiny ones that were in the beginning stages on various spots of his heels. It felt like a huge weight was lifted off of me to know that I had the help of nurses around the clock to help keep him turned and pain managed. My best efforts in caring for him at this stage wasn't enough. The staff made many remarks about how they were surprised that I drove him from Alabama by myself. These things were never at the forefront of my mind or heart. Hearing their remarks underscored how much God was my strength in getting to MD Anderson. I think the more I heard them recount how astounded they were, the more grateful I became that God was with me.

We learned that much of the large bedsore had become dead tissue, which can appear as the wound is healing. The doctors informed us that this dead tissue had to be removed because of bacteria that can form within it. We also found out that the bedsore was almost down to the bone, so the cleaning process would leave a deep gash once it was removed. The doctor arranged for a plastic surgeon to have a consultation with Qe because plastic surgery might be needed after the dead tissue was removed. Bed wound specialists came in around the clock to aid in cleaning and changing bandages. In between doctors and specialists coming in, Qe was surrounded by nurses laughing and conversing with him. Inwardly, I would laugh to myself as I would think about how much Qe was soaking up the love and attention from pretty nurses. He also became close friends with a couple of male nurses that quickly became a brotherhood and reflected an unbreakable bond.

After getting just a couple of hours of sleep, the first thing on my mind when I woke up the following morning was going to find the chapel. We would be receiving the report soon of Qe's new MRI results, and I needed to ask God for courage. I couldn't help but reflect on the name of this section of the hospital and the welcoming message that was on the white board that said "Welcome to the Mountains." In the Bible, monumental things happened on the mountain that all involved divine experiences with God. One thing I was sure of was that God had opened this door of opportunity for me and Qe. I wasn't fully sure of what all God's plan would be, but I knew He had a special plan. Qe and I talked about how it felt good to be away from home. Maybe it was the getting away from what was familiar that gave us the feeling that it was just us and God. I waited with eager anticipation to see what our mountain experience would be like during our time here.

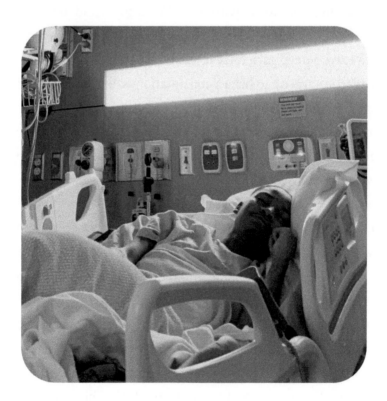

CHAPTER NINETEEN

GOD IS WITH US

Fear not, for I am with you; be not dismayed, for I am your God; I will strengthen you, I will help you, I will uphold you with my righteous right hand. — Isaiah 41:10 (ESV)

Many mornings, I sought a quiet spot to pray and calm my anxieties. I needed strength and wisdom from God for each moment, and God had never failed me. When it was time to be brave, I was brave, and when it was time to display faith, I stood in faith. I depended on God's strength to help me overcome my frailties that contradicted what I was believing God for. One morning, I grabbed a little breakfast from the cafeteria and headed back to Qe's room. When I walked in, he had the biggest smile on his face and a complete spread of food laid out before him that he'd ordered from the cafeteria. He said, "What's up, Ma?!" I chuckled and asked him if he liked the food, even though the answer was clear from the humongous smile on his face.

Qe was so excited about the menu options that he would read what they had to offer with great excitement. The food was all made to order, and the service could be compared to an upscale hotel. You can only imagine how much of a blessing this was, considering Qe's love for food. Hospital food is usually expected to be no one's favorite, and prior to this, it certainly hadn't been Qe's preference. Having food he enjoyed so readily available, removed the burden of me having to get meals outside of the hospital for him. But we still had intentions of taste-testing as much of Houston's food as possible before we left. One of Qe's favorite cuisines was seafood, and he was excited about trying H-Town's. It soon became a normal thing for the staff to walk in and see Qe holding the menu in his hand while intently staring at his food options. They would laugh and joke with Qe about his love for food. One nurse walked in and said, "Every time I come in you have that menu in your hand Q."

After a few days, my cousin Landress reached out to let me know that she had been anticipating hearing from me. She expected me to come by because she had a room prepared for me. I told her that I was trying to stay close to Qe because I was waiting to receive various results from scans and MRIs and ultimately, the plan doctors would suggest for Qe's care. Though all my reasons for staying close to the hospital were genuine, the truth was I didn't wish to impose either. Her heartfelt welcome quickly persuaded me. Landress had vivid memories of me as a child, but my only memory of her was hearing my mom speaking highly of her during my childhood years. After a few days, I finally pried myself away from Qe's side to go to my cousin's. When I arrived, she and her family welcomed me with open arms. Overwhelmed by her kindness, I became extremely comfortable being there. Her home instantly turned into my home away from home. Before leaving to come to Houston, some family and friends asked me who I knew or where I would stay if I needed such resources during my visit. When my response was that I didn't know and expressed my trust for God, I knew it created concern for them. But I quickly realized this was God's provision for me on this journey. Sleeping in a comfortable bed versus the small couch in Qe's hospital room gave me the rejuvenation I needed to make it from day to day. My routine shifted to driving back and forth between Cypress, TX, and MD Anderson in Houston, which was approximately a 45-minute drive with no traffic delays, and over an hour in their common heavy traffic.

I sought to balance my mood with whatever would bring me and Qe joy. I loved a good vibrant sunny day, and I began to wonder if the sun ever came out in Houston, TX. It was cloudy and rainy for days, and I craved seeing the sun shine down on us. Days turned into weeks before we realized it during our stay at MD Anderson. Every morning we received a visit from the team of doctors making their daily rounds. They made sure no new issues were arising in Qe's condition and that he was comfortable. Qe and I were both nervous about the first MRI results. This would tell us what kind of changes, if any, there had been in his tumors. The first MRI results revealed that there was only one small new spot on his spine. Doctors said that this was good considering the amount of time that had passed since he had received any treatments and the speed at which the cancer had spread previously.

No matter how small of a good report we received, I used it to fuel my hope. Weeks were passing by as the doctors took different measures to find a plan of care. They decided to perform a small biopsy to determine the activity of the cancer, but any surgery on his brain or spine was considered risky, so they decided to go in where the cancer originated, his right lung. These results didn't reveal any activity of cancer cells. We were glad to hear this, but it left the doctors puzzled because it didn't give them any insight on how to treat the cancer that existed in other areas of his body. Dr. Harrison said that it was great news that there weren't any active cancer cells where they performed the biopsy, but they couldn't make a plan off of cells with no cancer-like activity. The mystery remained of how to treat what existed on his brain and spine.

Qe and I grew close to a few of the doctors and nurses on the team. Their genuine concern and love was deeply heartfelt. Each day they reaffirmed that they were doing all they could to seek out the best treatment options. Dr. Brandon, a handsome young man in his early to mid-30s, is one who became like a friend. He exhibited wisdom beyond his years, and he had a kind and gentle spirit. I appreciated Dr. Brandon's youth in hopes that Qe would possibly rely on him as someone to talk to who seemed more like a peer to him. He would often come in and check on us even when he was assigned to a different area. Qe loved Dr. Brandon's sense of style and admirably complemented his attire one day as Dr. Brandon was leaving his room after a visit.

During my last trip to the mall with Qe, which was almost a year and a half prior to this moment, he talked about how he wanted to start dressing more professionally. He wanted his attire to reflect the level of success he planned to walk in, and one of Qe's aspirations was to build a profession within the medical field. As we were walking through the mall, he saw a red suede suit jacket that he rushed to. "I wanna start getting some jackets like this Ma!" He said as he was trying it on and posing. Qe'Vonte's compliments to Dr. Brandon reminded me of Qe's love for fashion and his professional goals. Since the past year had been filled with so much fight to save his life, this moment felt bittersweet because the future felt so uncertain.

Dr. Brandon and I would talk about the options he thought might be possible for Qe, but I could see the lack of hope in his eyes. I had seen this look many times before. He said there may be trial treatments or high intensity chemotherapy that might possibly be options, but everything was still being discussed; Dr. Harrison would have the ultimate decision. I told him that I understood but would remain hopeful. Qe had conquered cancer so many times prior to this. I was sure with God and their help, he could overcome it again. I appeared calm and confident on the outside, but inwardly my mother's heart was crying out for them to help me save my baby. In the meantime, other issues such as healing the severe bedsore, addressing his pain level, and physical therapy became the primary issues of concern. I was excited about these issues becoming a priority for the moment because they all ultimately played a part in improving Qe'Vonte's daily comfort.

They ordered Qe a sand bed which not only contributed to the healing and recovery of the pressure sores, but also increased his comfort. This was especially welcome, because he hadn't been able to get good rest for months. They also explained how the bed was designed to prevent new bedsores. Now we would not have to be as worried about him being in the bed as were before. Qe was assigned physical therapy, and they came daily to help him get out of bed. I was overjoyed because I struggled so much to do this when we were home. They taught him exercises to strengthen his upper body so that he would be able to better assist me in helping him get out of the bed when we got back home. Another objective was for him to regain as much independence as possible as a paraplegic. It had been discussed that even if his body was rid of the cancer, the doctors didn't know if he would ever be able to walk again. Qe would do pull-ups on the hospital bed trapeze and wheelchair push-ups each day. I saw his determination and will to fight in how he approached these activities.

One morning as I entered Qe's room, there was a keyboard piano on the floor. When I asked him about it, he said that music therapy had come by. It was such an adventure at MD Anderson. I can't express how happy my heart was to hear the words music therapy. Daily, I was surprised by how they provided the best of care during Qe's most challenging times. There was always a new activity or method of care that took Qe's mind off of his suffering and was perfectly aligned with his gifts and what he loved. Even when he was rusty, he loved playing over and over to perfect it. Now he had someone else that he could show off his talent to with the added benefit of it being therapy. I also began to see an assortment of drawings beginning to collect on his table and around the room. Even if he was coloring or drawing just to pass the time, it made my heart smile because all forms of art were appreciated by both of us. By the way, we were on the children's floor of the hospital because neuroblastoma was considered a "childhood" cancer. The children's floor was amazing! There were fun surprises happening almost everyday. Sometimes visitors even stopped by to offer freshly baked cookies or other yummy treats.

Another astounding individual that quickly won our hearts was Ms. Jo, who was a nurse practitioner. She gained the nickname "my forever friend" over the course of our time there. I always told her that she had a spicy personality, and she'd often respond with laughter or a reminder that she was ex-military. She was all about defending people who could not fight for themselves. I knew she was a person who tried to make a difference in the lives of all the patients she came in contact with. Her sincere love and kindness became an anchor for me when things became overwhelming. It felt good to have someone to lean on in such a way.

Jo often expressed how much she had fallen in love with Qe's smile and personality. Qe had become like a superstar on that 9th floor, and Ms. Jo was his biggest fan. It felt as if she made herself available to us around the clock. It helped me a great deal to be able

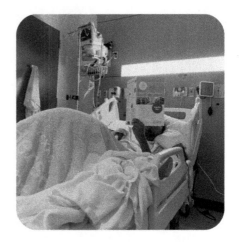

to text or call her about any concerns I had. Jo helped us in so many various ways, from covering my daily parking fees to bringing Qe loads of candy and snacks for the weekends she wasn't there.

Qe's relationship with all of his nurses was golden. There was a sweet little nurse that had been his morning nurse the majority of the time. Nichole played a big part in helping us feel comfortable. She would cheerfully come in and greet him in the mornings at the beginning of her shift. One day, he responded "Yeaaah dude," to one of her questions. I immediately interjected with the serious mama tone, "Qe, don't call her a dude! Be respectful." Nichole quickly interjected to let me know that he was fine and that she wasn't offended at all because that's how they talked to each other. He was like, "Yeah Ma, we cool." Never seeing Qe interact with a nurse or professional this way definitely caught me by surprise. We all laughed as she continued on with her conversation with Qe and daily routine of care for him. There were so many people that were like angels gifted to us, and it strengthened my heart to know that God was with us.

CHAPTER
TWENTY

HE'S ALL WE NEED

On Jan 26th, I headed to the hospital from my cousin's house. I grabbed something to eat on the way as I looked forward to hanging with Qe for a few hours. After I arrived and got settled, he sadly told me that Kobe Bryant had died, along with his daughter. I was at a loss for words at the news. As we discussed our disbelief and shock regarding the accident, Qe said, "Ma, I can't believe this man lost his life just like that, and here I am here fighting for my life all this time and have managed to make it this far." I reiterated to him that our times are in God's hands and that is why we must keep trusting God. My intention was to remind him that God had a purpose for his life and was in total control.

After about a month of Qe being hospitalized, I was becoming concerned about getting back to Kayla. So I decided to start traveling back and forth from Alabama to Houston. I would go to work a couple of weeks and then drive back to spend the weekend with Qe. Ms. Jo offered her full support to watch over him while I was gone. I trusted she would look after him as intently as I would —it comforted my mama's heart. We also had the support of my cousin.

Treatment options began to look promising for Qe once Dr. Harrison found a couple of hospitals that were offering clinical trials specifically for neuroblastoma. The clinical trials were being given in New York at Memorial Sloan Kettering and Indiana Children's Hospital. Dr. Harrisons' first plan was to ask if the medicine could be administered to Qe at MD Anderson. If that wasn't an option, he asked if we were willing to travel to one of those hospitals if they accepted him into their trial program. My answer was definitely yes. I did not know how I was going to do it, but I was determined.

Dr. Harrison reached out to Memorial Sloan Kettering Cancer Center in New York first, and as we waited to hear back from them, I started my journey back home to Alabama. Kayla was heavy on my heart, and I knew she probably missed us. I looked forward to spending time with her and giving her my undivided attention since I had been so laser focused on her brother. My mind had also been on maintaining my position at my job, since I had only been there for a few months. Even though my bosses were very understanding, I didn't want to risk losing my position. After the 11-hour drive, I headed straight to Kayla to surprise her because I didn't tell her I was coming home. She had just gotten her hair done at Boniechia's hair salon and was curled up in a chair with her face in her phone. I ran into the shop to surprise her before she could see me, and she leaped up from her seat in surprise and tears began to flow. We embraced each other as our tears turned into laughter.

Going back to work while Qe was in Texas was challenging for me mentally and emotionally. I did my best to maintain my composure at work because much of the time my mind was on Qe. He had also started having headaches again, and sometimes he wouldn't tell the nurses. Because of this, I stayed in contact with Jo when he mentioned that he was having headaches or any sort of pains. Valentine's Day was quickly approaching, and I was planning my drive back to Houston. This would be a good time to take Kayla to see Qe since I was only going back for a few days and returning. Their dad rode along as well, saving me from driving in the dark rainy weather, since we started our drive around 1 am. I was grateful he came. The last four hours I drove, he and Kayla went back and forth playing their favorite R&B '90s songs, laughing and singing along.

During the ride there, Qe texted me to say how excited he was to see all of us, and when we all walked in his room, a joyous smile came over his face. I gave him space and time with his dad and sister since he hadn't seen them in a while. There were all sorts of cards, candies, and gifts lying around his room that hospital staff had brought to him since it was the day before Valentine's Day. I worked on organizing his room and sorting his things into storage bins as he laughed and talked to his dad and sister.

The first major decision we had to make was what kind of local Houstonian food to eat. I was not surprised when seafood won the vote because Qe and Kayla got their love for seafood from their dad. This Valentine's Day was special because we were all there together with Qe to shower him with our love and support. Xzavier called and I passed the phone around for him to talk to everyone. He enjoyed hearing everyone's voices, especially his brother's. On the fourth day, we headed back to Alabama, eagerly anticipating a call regarding which clinical trial would be made available.

One evening right before I was about to go to bed, Qe and I were texting each other about our day and getting ready to say our good nights when he texted me saying "God is really good just to let us see this many days together." I paused to take in what he was really saying to me because it didn't feel good to read these words. I stared at my phone a moment and then responded "God has the last word over your life and to have peace. Love you son." But that night I tossed and turned because I knew my son was telling me goodbye in the most subtle and sweet way. I just couldn't accept that in my heart. I couldn't stop the tears from flowing throughout the night as I silently cried.

Finally, a response was received from New York. They declined Qe for the clinical trial due to his age. Qe was 23 and the trial was for 18 years old and younger. The same report came back from the children's hospital in Indiana as well. I was devastated, and it felt like a nightmare to know there was some type of medication that could help him get better while at the same time being denied access to it. Dr. Harris even reached out to the company that made the trial medicine to see if they could send it to MD Anderson for him to administer it to Qe, but there were technicalities that didn't allow that as well. During this period, I worked for almost three weeks before I received a message from Jo that the doctors needed to speak with me. Text messages began to slow down tremendously from Qe. He rarely texted me back and my good morning texts had almost come to a complete halt. It immediately reminded me of the time period in November when he was hospitalized, and he had pulled back from everyone.

When they called, I stepped away from my work desk to go outside. Dr. Moody began to go over things that we had previously discussed. She went on to say that Qe hadn't been feeling well due to the frequent headaches and that they had done a scan of his head. The scan revealed that the tumor at the base of his brain had grown slightly and was likely the cause for the headaches. She also expressed that Qe had become very withdrawn and quiet and wanted to know how quickly I could make it back to Houston to be with him. I left that night accompanied by Kayla and Robert. We arrived the next day at 1:30 pm. My heart was saddened when I thought about him suffering in silence. As we walked into his room, he spoke to his dad and sister and then looked up at me and said, "Hey Ma" with a grin that was dimmer than usual. But he appeared to be joyful that we had made it. The doctor's only suggestion at this stage was that radiation could possibly shrink the tumor to help relieve pressure; however, this wasn't considered as a way of healing him but only a way to ease his suffering.

That evening, I asked him what he wanted to eat. The nurse told me that he really hadn't eaten much for the past few days. He pondered for a moment and murmured, "Hmmmm, I can go for some shrimp Alfredo." When his dad and I got back with his food, Qe was asleep and only took a couple of very small bites. The radiation doctor came to speak with us regarding the risks and possible side effects associated with radiating the same area again. One thing was for certain: if we did not radiate, Qe would experience excruciating headaches. We all agreed on small amounts of radiation. Due to the urgency, the doctor scheduled treatments to start that evening. Robert and Kayla remained in the room as the hospital staff escorted Qe for treatment. The hospital was drafty, so I hung close to Qe to cover him up each time the covers slipped off. They parked his bed outside the radiation room. As we waited, I began to talk to him about what was happening back home in an attempt to distract him. After a couple of minutes, he looked at me solemnly and with a half-smile and said, "Ma, I really would like for it to be quiet right now."

I immediately apologized as I backed away to my seat on the other side of the hall. I can honestly say that I had never received that type of response from him, so I was somewhat taken aback. Soon after the radiation technician came out and took Qe back to the radiation room. As I sat there in that hallway thinking about his chilling response, I became overwhelmed with sadness. I began to cry uncontrollably. A young man that had stopped to check on me and Qe several times walked over to me and knelt down to console me. He kept saying, "Mama, it's going to be alright. It's going to be alright. I know it's hard. You've done all that you can do now and the rest is in God's hands." I could only nod as I attempted to stop crying but couldn't. He walked away while still assuring me that everything was going to be okay. That night and the following day, Qe slept. Late that afternoon, I began to feel like Qe had been asleep much longer than usual, but everyone said that he was just tired from the new pain medication and radiation. I initially planned for me and Kayla to spend the night at my cousin's house that evening, but something in my heart led me to believe we should stay close by overnight. So I went to the front desk to ask about the Ronald McDonald House room availability options. The front desk said they usually wouldn't have a room available at such a short notice but miraculously one was available. Since I was exhausted, I decided to go straight to the room to take a nap and check on Qe later that night.

At midnight, I went to check on him, and he was still asleep, which alarmed me because I knew in my heart that Qe wouldn't sleep this long no matter how much medication he had received. I started calling his name to wake him up to ease my concern. "Qe... Qe!... Qe'Vonte!" I called. I gently shook him and called him again. He slightly opened his eyes and muttered "Huuuh". I knew that something wasn't right. I did it again and recorded him to show the doctors how he wasn't really responding. I texted Jo immediately apologizing for texting so late but that I was deeply disturbed because something was wrong with Qe. Soon the technicians were coming in to take him for scans. I went back to my room, curled up on the bed, and mustered up the strength to pray. When I thought my soul couldn't experience more distress, it did. I fell asleep and was soon awakened by a call from Robert telling me to come back to the room because the doctor was there with results.

When I walked in the room, Qe eyes were open, gazing toward the ceiling. He looked disoriented. I could tell by the doctor's face he didn't have good news for us. I sat down and braced myself for the conversation. I remember tensing up, reminding myself that...

whatever comes out of his mouth, God is bigger. But I knew that whatever he shared would be another blow to my heart. Quite frankly I can't remember what the doctor said before the main brunt of the news came. He said that the tumor at the base of Qe's brain was hemorrhaging. He went on to say that if the tumor was any place else in the body, normal protocol would be to perform emergency surgery, but with it being at the base of the brain the risk was high for permanent damage to his lungs or heart, or he could be left in a vegetative state afterwards. He even said that he may only have as much as 24 hours to live. At some point while the doctor talked, I just started shaking my head to all the things that he said could possibly happen as tears ran down my face. *No*. My "no" was to answer the questions he was asking which was whether we wanted them to risk doing the surgery.

Qe could barely talk, so I had to answer for him. After all that he'd been through, I knew he would not want to endure a brain surgery with this magnitude of risk. I had seen him sign the DNR order twice and heard him say "Just let me be" when asked by the doctors if he would like to be resuscitated if at any time he stopped breathing. I was clear about what Qe's wishes were. After the doctor left the room, I walked over to the side of Qe's bed and called his name. His eyes were open but slightly unfocused. He softly answered, "Hmm." I said, "Did you hear what the doctor said baby?" He answered yes with a gentle *mmhmm*. I repeated what the doctor said just to make sure Qe heard and understood. I couldn't stop myself from crying as I spoke to him. After repeating the doctor's report, I said, "Qe, all we got is God" and he responded, "...and that's all we need." His words pierced my soul as

I cried, and I began to pray aloud letting God know that we still trusted Him.

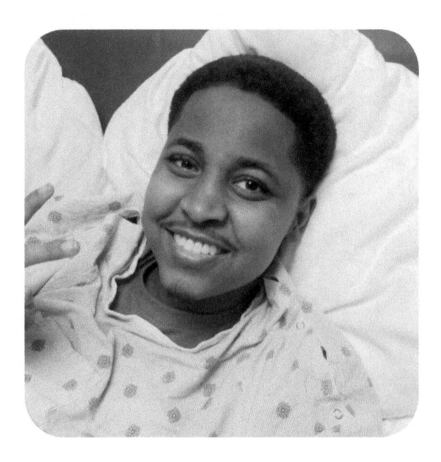

CHAPTER
TWENTY-ONE

REST

I t was 4 am. I rushed to wake Kayla so she could come visit Qe. She was sleeping with me in the Ronald McDonald room down the hall. I wasn't sure how a hemorrhaging tumor would affect him cognitively. We were already starting to notice his speech decline. When I woke Kayla, I told her Qe wasn't doing well and she needed to come see him. My heart grieved heavily for Kayla. I couldn't fathom how she was processing the weight of what we were walking through. When she approached his bedside, they gave each other the biggest hug and expressed how much they loved each other. Kayla wept heavily as she almost laid across his body. Qe also said to his dad, "Hey Dad, give me a five," as he extended his hand toward his dad. Little did we know, those words would be his last. Almost immediately after this, Qe fell asleep, and we gave him space so he could rest. I sent a text to our family and friends letting them know that Qe's condition was declining. I asked everyone again to pray for a miracle. I could not let go of this beautiful life that God had entrusted into my care.

Watching Qe suffer brought me excruciating pain and just when I thought the burden of my pain couldn't get any worse, it did. I went back to my room, and I cried as I prayed, begging God to please reconsider if it was His decision to take Qe. Reaching a point where I couldn't even speak because I was at a complete loss for words, I could only lament. I called my pastor to share the grave news, and as always, her words comforted me in my darkest hour and her wisdom enlightened me. All I could ever imagine was Qe's will to live, not that he would ever desire to rest from life. It's something I don't believe any parent would ever naturally imagine. I reflected on how he had told my pastor that he had lived a long life. It was hard for me to embrace his truth. My love for him could only fight for and embrace life for him, not death. I gained a greater understanding of Qe'Vonte's truth as I opened my heart up more in attempts to see his journey from his point of view. It was a painful truth. I remembered him saying many times when asked about his cancer journey, "I've had cancer as long as I can remember—all my life." The pain he endured was emotional, psychological, and physical. I realized even more clearly that his pain was much different from my own.

I was coming into a new understanding of the moment we were in, and beginning to realize that my faith had been so fueled by my unconditional love that I had become blind to how tired he had truly become. I was convinced God would heal him completely and grant Qe relief. I never foresaw or considered that Qe's story would include a chapter in which his life would end before my own. As a mother, this felt unnatural and incomprehensible. I reflected on my faith and how I had believed God for him to live for 15 years…and now, what do I do with my faith? What do I believe in if Qe is leaving despite my faith and prayers? As these thoughts raced through my head, I felt God impress on my heart that the same faith I had for so many years to hold on to his life was not wasted. It was the same faith I would need to let him go. The time had come for me to release my son into God's hands.

God was gently holding my hand through what would be the hardest moment of my life yet. He had made an executive decision that would override my deepest desire for my son. I again looked for comfort in God's word, as I toiled with the pain and grief within my soul. I was reminded of Jesus in the garden of Gethsemane when He prayed, "Father, if you are willing, take this cup from me; yet not my will, but yours be done" Luke 22:42 (NIV). He knew the time was drawing near for his greatest moment of suffering which would lead to his death as He said this prayer to the Father. In my own state of agony, my heart was slowly accepting God's will over my own…as I watched my son dying. I reflected on Jesus' agonizing moment in the garden as He prayed that God would remove His own cup of suffering, yet yielded to it by praying, "not my will but your will be done."

That morning when he closed his eyes to take what I thought was a nap, I had no idea it would be the last time he'd be able to interact with us. Throughout the day, Qe would sometimes gently squeeze our hand when he heard his name. Sometimes we could see small reactions in his facial expressions that made us feel like he was trying to respond. There was nothing more the doctors could do because they didn't have a way to stop the tumor from bleeding. It was suspected that the tumor began to bleed either because the radiation irritated it or because it had run out of room in the skull to expand any further. At a moment when I felt I was near the end of what I could handle, I received a call from one of my dear friends, Knegleshia. As she expressed her concern for our family, I began to tell her that I felt like this was all too much for me to bear. She graciously and confidently responded, "But you are bearing it—God is holding you up right now." She was one of my fellow warriors of faith, and her words strengthened me to continue walking through what felt terrifying.

I had not seen Kayla for some time, so I decided to go look for her. There was a small kitchen sitting area for families on that floor where I found Kayla head down, crying. I went in to console her as I struggled to find words of comfort. I began to apologize to her for being helpless to shield her from this pain. She began to comfort me and tell me I had nothing to apologize for because it wasn't my fault. I was trying my best to be her rock, as I was crumbling myself. The mama bear in me wanted desperately to protect her from this pain, but I stood powerless.

Sometimes I would talk to Qe and I'd see a tear form in the corner of his eye. My soul was being crushed to know that we were at the last moments of his life and not able to speak to each other. In my agony, I asked God why He was being mean to me. It felt cruel to me at that moment to not be able to hear him speak back to me or look at me. I knew Qe was in there trying to communicate with us, but couldn't. Every morning, I pulled up a chair up to his bedside and to hold his hand, talk to him, and pray.

One morning as I was driving to the hospital, I was having a difficult time understanding why God was allowing this, and again I prayed with all of my brokenness laid out before God. I struggled to accept Qe leaving us. At that moment, God impressed on my heart and said to me, "Do you think it is only my plan for you to keep tirelessly fighting this battle? Am I not a God that also gives my people rest? Therefore, I am giving both of you rest." I knew that God was referencing our fight for his life all 15 years. Fighting had become my default because anything else was a form of surrendering to cancer. He was ready to give us rest. I thought not to question His sovereignty but to accept this was His will and purpose for us. At that moment, "Tell Me Where It Hurts" by Fred Hammond began to play on the radio. The words were as if God Himself was singing to me. The love of God was comforting me in my deepest pain.

With this new enlightenment and understanding of rest, it was as if a light bulb turned on within my soul. I urgently needed to get to Qe to talk to him. I did not want him to leave this earth without his ears hearing me give him a proper release, and that I had found peace to release him. Something within me knew that I had arrived at a place that Qe had been praying for me to get to. I needed him to hear me say that it was ok for him to rest and that I would be ok. I didn't want him to leave this earth without him hearing me say this. It was also in this moment that I realized more than ever before that his transitioning from this life to the next was not a defeat or loss in his battle with cancer, but that it was God giving Qe'Vonte rest. After parking in the hospital garage, I raced to his room with this revelation. I anxiously entered his room, ran by his bedside and grabbed his hand. I said, "Qe! You can let go now. God told me that He was giving you rest!" Saying goodbye pained my heart, but then I thought about one day, by the grace of God, I'll see him in Heaven. Then I said to him, "I'll see you again my son! You can rest! It's ok! You can rest son!"

To my surprise, Qe nodded his head up and down one good time letting me know that he heard me. He had not shown any physical sign like that in days. I wept as I rubbed his chest and held his hand, letting him know I would make sure his sister and brother would be ok. I assured him that the strength that he said I had...I would use it to be strong. Whatever I could say to give his soul peace, I said. Afterward, I went to reposition myself on the other side of his bed in my chair to hold his hand. My eyes happened to land on the white board that the nurses and staff wrote on. The word "Rest" was written on the board in big letters. I couldn't help but smile, knowing it was my confirmation. This understanding of God giving us rest gave me peace to let go but it did not ease the agony in my soul. My grief was great.

Qe's oxygen levels had dropped, so they put him on a ventilator. Now we turned our attention to his heart monitor, as we knew his time was drawing near. The doctors explained to us what signs may occur right before Qe's last breath, but they also explained that everyone is different. After a little over seven days, Robert said he needed to return to work and decided to head back to Alabama. Kayla decided to leave with him as well. When I asked her if she really wanted to stay, she said that she knew there was nothing more she could do as she looked sadly over at her brother. They asked me if I was sure I was okay to stay by myself. I was at peace with being alone with Qe. It almost felt nostalgic because so much of our journey had involved being alone together at the hospital. However, I was also a bit uneasy. Covid-19 was brewing in the background, and society was adjusting as businesses began to close their doors. I prepared myself to be shut in with Qe, no longer traveling back and forth between my cousin's home and the hospital.

After they began their journey back home, I embraced the silence. The only sounds were his heart monitor and the ventilator. As I washed his face in the mornings, I hoped that he would look up at me and smile one more time. One day as I sat in the room alone with Qe, one of the doctors came in to visit. This particular doctor was kind and special to our journey. He once told me and Qe that he didn't really believe in God, but that he definitely believed that a supernatural power brought us to the hospital. He began by saying that he was so sorry to hear about Qe's decline. He talked about how special Qe was and about Qe's smile. He asked me how I was doing. As I attempted to describe what was happening in my head and heart, I made a comment about not knowing where to place my hope since my son was leaving me. My faith and hope had only prepared for him to live, but I did not know how to direct my hope in his dying state.

He said, "Well, it's not that we stop having hope, but that we change what we have hope for." This was another enlightening moment in my darkness. His words helped me to understand that I did not have to lose my hope for Qe but to redirect it. The hope that carried me through all the disappointments throughout this journey gave me strength. I didn't know what to do with hope now that my Qe was leaving me. We went on to talk about where we would place our hope now…which was that in Qe's final days, he would have peace and not be in any discomfort or pain.

I played "Tell Me Where It Hurts" for us as I put one AirPod in his ear and I had the other in my ear. The words of this beautiful song comforted me, knowing we could go to our Father in heaven and tell Him where we are hurting. I found peace in the knowledge that He would fix it because He is the God that heals. I played this song on repeat as I hoped that the words brought Qe as much peace as it did to me. I held my son's hand while eternity held the other.

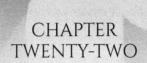

CHAPTER
TWENTY-TWO

CHANGING CLOTHES

As I grieved heavily in Qe's final days, holding his hand by his bedside each morning, I didn't share the magnitude of my pain with many. I could only talk to Qe briefly before I became overwhelmed with grief. I promised him that I would share his story, take care of his siblings, and take care of myself because I knew this is what he cared about the most.

Dr. Moody came into our room one morning and sat down with me at the table. Like so many of the staff that had come to offer their support and share fond memories of Qe, she spoke of the tremendous impact Qe made on her and the staff during his time there. I shared my concern about him suffering, but she said that she believed Qe's awareness may have been that of an infant's. I didn't believe that was completely accurate because Qe's facial reactions were strong when I washed his face. She appeared to be shocked when I shared this and asked me to demonstrate. I warmed a towel and went over to his bedside. She began talking to Qe as she held his hand as I began to wash his face. His eyes and lips tightened as if to make it easier to wipe around them.

Dr. Moody was so astounded that she asked me if she could record him to show the team of doctors. They would discuss whether it was best to take him off the ventilator because this meant that he could possibly be suffering and unable to communicate. After a few hours, she came back accompanied by a few other staff members that had grown close to our family. Dr. Moody informed me that the doctors felt it would be best to take him off the ventilator. All I could think of is what Qe would want. I knew if he could talk he would say "Just let me be" as he had expressed when he signed the DNR papers on two occasions. My love outweighed any thoughts that contradicted what I knew he wanted. Throughout this journey, I'd often tell him that I only wanted him to have the very best, especially when it came to certain decisions that required personal sacrifices. I knew I had to to choose what was best for him at this moment.

The doctors told me and his dad that he would not recover from this state and that it would be best to take him off the ventilator. As painful as it was, we agreed, and that evening Dr. Moody came back accompanied by Jo and a couple of nurses to ease him off the ventilator. Though my heart was crushed, I had a sense of peace knowing this was the decision Qe would make. Dr. Moody held Qe's hand and spoke to him about taking him off the ventilator. He laid there as he had been for the last nine days and we weren't sure if he understood or even heard us. I was holding his other hand with tears flowing down my face.

His ventilator was pumping over eighty percent oxygen into his body, and she began to slowly take it down...seventy...sixty... and so on, until it was completely off. His breathing was already strained, and none of us knew what to expect once it was completely shut off. We all braced ourselves. It was as if everything moved in slow motion. I felt numb. When the ventilator went off, stillness and quietness filled the room all except for Qe's strained raspy breaths. They all stayed in the room for about ten more minutes, knowing he could take his last breath at any moment. As they slowly exited the room with saddened demeanors, Dr. Moody told me to let them know if I needed anything.

It was about 7:30 pm. I scooted as close as I could to Qe, holding his hand as I watched his chest go up and down with every single breath. There was one particular moment in which I thought he inhaled his last breath. His chest became completely still... nothing. I looked at him intently and wondered, *is this it?* Then he inhaled. That long pause between breaths felt like time had stopped, and I believed I had stopped breathing as well. I wondered if every breath was his last. No matter the cost, I had dedicated myself to be by his side throughout the entire battle because I never wanted him to feel alone, even until his final breath (which I never thought would come because I always imagined that one day he would bury me).

One doctor that I had never met before came to check on us late that night. She gave her condolences while looking over at Qe's heart monitor and said, "You have a fighter right here." She was amazed at how long he had been in his current state since the tumor had started hemorrhaging. I smiled as I witnessed Qe defying the odds even in his very last hours of life, which testified that God was in control and that Qe was truly a warrior.

My cousin came to sit with me that night. She knew how exhausted I was and urged me to get some rest while she watched Qe for me. Though I was extremely exhausted, I could only doze off for a few minutes at a time sporadically. As I lay on the couch next to Qe's bed, listening to each labored breath, it was impossible to rest. It was about 11 pm when I assured her that she could leave because I wasn't going to be able to sleep. I tossed, turned, and cried as I listened to his strained breathing for the remainder of the night. Not knowing what his level of awareness was or if he could feel pain from his struggle to breathe tore my heart into pieces. At one point I begged God to go ahead and take him. Every strained raspy breath ripped through my soul. I turned on gospel music to help soothe me, and I finally fell asleep at some point in the night, waking up early the next morning extremely exhausted. I decided to go to my cousin's house to take a shower to refresh myself for what I would have to endure emotionally that day. I asked my friend Jo if she could sit with Qe while I did so. I felt a sense of release from the tight grip that I had held on to his life. I believe inwardly I had reached some sense of surrendering his life into God's hand.

Days prior, I had been preparing my mind to remember what the Bible said about death, so I would be prepared emotionally once Qe transitioned. I would tell myself, *remember Rose, his body is just the house his spirit lives in; his spirit is going home to be with God.* It was as if I was rehearsing the moment because I didn't want to faint or my sanity to collapse because it all felt so surreal. My son was dying.

> *For we know that when this earthly tent we live in is taken down (that is, when we die and leave this earthly body), we will have a house in heaven, an eternal body made for us by God himself and not by human hands. We grow weary in our present bodies, and we long to put on our heavenly bodies like new clothing. For we will put on heavenly bodies; we will not be spirits without bodies. While we live in these earthly bodies, we groan and sigh, but it's not that we want to die and get rid of these bodies that clothe us. Rather, we want to put on our new bodies so that these dying bodies will be swallowed up by life. God himself has prepared us for this, and as a guarantee he has given us his Holy Spirit. So we are always confident, even though we know that as long as we live in these bodies we are not at home with the Lord. For we live by believing and not by seeing. Yes, we are fully confident, and we would rather be away from these earthly bodies, for then we will be at home with the Lord.*
> —*2 Corinthians 5:1-8 (NLT)*

Once I arrived at my cousin's, I freshened up and did my best to take in something to eat for strength and began heading back to the hospital. The drive gave me time to meditate and pray. I had braced myself as much as I could for what the day would hold. When I exited the elevators onto the 9th floor and turned the corner of the hallway, his room was the first in my line of sight. I saw Ms. Jo standing outside his room with a solemn look on her face. At that moment I knew he was gone. As I approached, I smiled at her as if to say, I know he's gone, and it's okay. She told me that Qe had passed away a few minutes before I arrived, at 11:22 am. It was March 17, 2020.

As I entered the room, Ms. Jo and the chaplain stood there with their gazes fixed on me, watching for my reaction. I felt numb...*I'm okay*, I thought. I walked over by the foot of his bed, and he looked like he was sleeping. No more labored breathing, no more beeps from the heart monitor. The room was quiet. My phone began to ring and it was Xzavier. It was as if he knew. I asked them to excuse me while I broke the news to his brother. His first response after a short pause was, "Oh..ok, I'm ok," as if he was trying to process the news. I hated that we couldn't be together during this time, so I could comfort him with my hugs and just be in the company of each other. I expressed how much I loved him and told him to call me as much as he needed. Before I reached out to anyone, I stood at the foot of Qe's bed, paralyzed for a moment.

I rehearsed the spiritual truth I had been meditating on, which was his spirit was with God now, and this was just the body that served as a house for the real Qe'Vonte. I needed all of God and the truth of His Word to continue moving forward. It was the only thing that gave me the strength to endure such loss. The chaplain walked over to me and said they had something for me. She pulled out a small box as she explained that it was a gift the hospital wanted to give me. It was a heart necklace consisting of two individual hearts, a smaller heart nested inside of a larger heart with two small strings. She said that the smaller heart was to tie around Qe's wrist, and the bigger heart was for me to wear as a necklace. She said it was a symbol of our love and we would always be connected. I burst into tears as reality began to set in.

Having to tell Kayla was heavy on my heart. She's the youngest in the family, and I watched her believe for a miracle with such innocence and bravery. I didn't know how to address the pain that she would experience and felt helpless knowing the tremendous grief she was about to carry. I FaceTimed her to see her face as I broke the news. She cried out, "Noooo Mama, nooooo. I want my brother...Let me see him, I want to see him!" Through tear-filled eyes, all I could say was "I'm sorry Kayla...I'm so sorry."

The nurses asked if I wanted to give him his last bath, and I declined. I felt like David must have felt after begging God to save his son once they informed him that he had died. David got up from the floor, washed himself, put lotion on, and changed his clothes. Then he went into the Lord's house to worship. I had accepted God's divine will and was ready to go home after a long battle. Though I was heartbroken, I knew Qe was more alive than ever before now that he was in the presence of God.

> *Then David got up from the ground, washed himself, put on lotions, and changed his clothes. He went to the Tabernacle and worshiped the Lord. After that, he returned to the palace and was served food and ate. —2 Samuel 12:20 (NLT)*

Jo helped me move my belongings into a room labeled "Family Room." As I started to prepare to go home, a nurse asked me if the staff could pay their respects to Qe. I thought it would be an honor, and I graciously allowed it. As doctors, nurses, and staff came to pay their respects, they would come to my room and hug me and share with me how Qe was such an amazing young man and impacted their lives greatly. This was just the beginning of my son's sweet legacy unfolding before my eyes. They paid homage to Qe like he was a king and it blessed my heart. I was fortunate to get a glimpse of how many friends he had made at MD Anderson and the lives he touched while he was there.

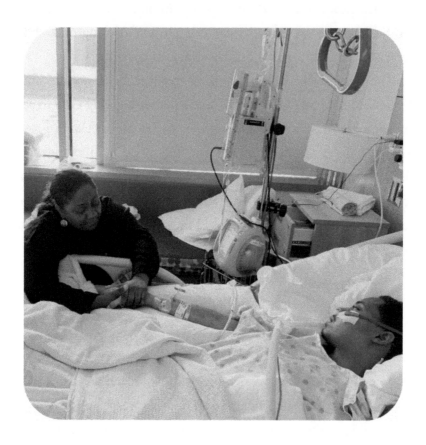

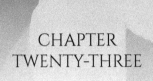

CHAPTER
TWENTY-THREE

Triumphant Love

*And now abide faith, hope, love, these three; but the
greatest of these is love. —1 Corinthians 13:13 (NKJV)*

As I drove away from the hospital, I wondered if at some point in my journey I lacked faith or did something wrong to receive the outcome I was facing. It was then that I felt God impress on my heart that faith is not only receiving what I have asked for, but faith is what carries me in times I don't receive what I want. My perspective of faith was being refined. Faith triumphs when it exists in each facet of our life's journey. Just as I had faith to hold on to Qe, I had to have faith to let go. Now I had to walk by faith that God would carry me through this season of grief. Qe's beautiful smile became the face of his legacy, and his love transformed people's lives. It was his determination to smile beyond his pain that people remembered most.

We encountered many valleys throughout this journey. Qe struggled at times with feelings of defeat, depression, and hopelessness. There were times he wanted his life to end because of the pain, and he wondered if he would be remembered if he died. The battle caused me to experience periods of deep sadness, helplessness, and unforeseen challenges of all kinds. God was using this trial to strengthen me and stretch my faith. It brought me into a broader understanding of what faith truly is and to understand it has no limitations. Some of my darkest nights were watching Qe suffer from an illness that eventually separated us in this life. This tribulation I reference as a time I sat in darkness, but the Lord was my radiant light.

> *Though I sit in darkness, the Lord will be my light.*
> —*Micah 7:8 (NIV)*

Qe shared encouraging words with others during times he needed encouragement himself. God's light and love shining through him is what we remembered most because it was the core of who he was, not the battles he wrestled with on the outside. Legacy was unfolding before my eyes, and I couldn't have been more proud to hear stories surface from friends, family, and strangers of how Qe had made a positive impact on their lives.

One of Qe's dearest mentors and cherished friends, Jemeana Roberson shared,

> *Qe'Vonte was one of the most positive people someone could have ever met. I had the pleasure of teaching him as his Bible youth teacher. He was energetic, welcoming, attentive, and respectful. He had a smile that could brighten any dark room or even chase away negative feelings. You could not be around Qe'Vonte without laughing. He was hilarious. I never grew tired of hearing stories about his life issues or struggles in school. He had such a way with words that his mere*

presence could put you at ease.

I remember when I was recovering from an illness that weakened my legs. With difficulties to stand or even walk, Knowing about my condition, Qe'Vonte encouraged me by saying, "Mrs. Jemeana, come on and run right now. We are not going to accept this report! Come and chase me in the parking lot right now! Come on, run, and catch me." I thought he was out of his mind, but his voice was so assuring that I ran, pushing my legs to their limit. Qe'Vonte shouted as he ran between the cars in the church parking lot, "That's it! Run, come and get me! The devil is a liar! Come on now!" I ran with tears forming in my eyes, feeling the pain with every step, but I did it because of Qe'Vonte. What a motivator he was!

Despite his health condition, Qevonte would never display defeat or any downcast attitude. He would continuously speak about the goodness of God, reaffirming his faith. Qevonte was a fighter! He fought to the end, never relinquishing his faith in God. "I want to live!" he would always say to me as his cancer became more aggressive. Even when he lost his ability to walk, he would still praise God, even though he was in excruciating pain.

I am so glad that Qevonte does not have to fight any longer. I believe he is at rest now with the Lord. Thessalonians 4:14 says, "For since we believe that Jesus died and rose again, even so, through Jesus, God will bring with him those who have fallen asleep." He will no longer be ill from any radiation treatments and medicines. He will no longer be exhausted and financially strained from doctor visits. He will no longer have to endure the pain and shame of his strength being impaired or being unable to function under debilitating pain. Qevonte, my student, my friend, I miss you. Hopefully soon, we will run again together, free of pain and illness. Thank you, Qevonte, for everything.

Qe lived 15 years after being diagnosed with neuroblastoma at the age of eight with a life expectancy of five years. Qe lived nine months after the doctors said he would only have six months to live. Qe lived 10 days after the report that he may only have 24 hours to live. God granted us time and more time throughout this journey. This was God's goodness toward us along with every other treasure He allowed to bloom in our darkness. Take a moment to reflect on the blessings blooming in the midst of what might be a dark season in your life.

Qe was a fighter and God knows that even warriors need rest. In the midst of a broken heart, I found joy in the fact that Qe was now resting from all the troubles of this world. God gifted me with three children I love with everything in me, but God is in charge of the length of their days.

Children are a gift from the Lord; they are a reward from him. —*Psalm 127:3 (NLT)*

Qe'Vonte,

My dear son, I am so proud of the man that you grew to become. I choose to give thanks for the time we were given. I have learned my most precious lessons about God and faith from being on the frontline of your many battles. Fighting for you has taught me my greatest lessons of what God's unconditional love is toward all of His children.

God did not fail us, but He promoted you to live with Him for all eternity. Your faith fought for me at the end when you held on as long as you could just to make sure we would be okay. Your love was selfless and I want you to know that I see you as victorious. Victory comes in many different forms, and you have overcome cancer and all of the darkness of this world by receiving God's second chance that was offered through Christ Jesus. That is the reason we can rejoice! Qe, I will see you again, my beautiful boy! I have promised you that I will be ok, and that's what I have applied my faith toward now.

I am pressing toward the mark of the higher calling son. To tell your story...our story of faith that both our pain and our purpose may shine light in someone else's darkness. I know your smile is shining bright in heaven. Your smile will continue to light my path as I journey through this life, but I know that we are forever spiritually connected in Christ.

Until I see you again...
Mom

ABOUT THE AUTHOR

Rosemary Sherrod was born and raised in Chicago but for the past 21 years has made her home in Huntsville, Alabama. In her professional life, she is a successful graphic designer and web developer. Additionally, after over 20 years of serving in an active role within her church, she recently became an ordained minister.

The turbulent times she's experienced throughout her life include the death of her son Qe'Vonte from cancer. This compelled her to write her book, Believing in the Dark, chronicling his fifteen year battle with the disease. She hopes this story will be used to uplift, enlighten, and inspire people to love their lives fully through God.

Today, Rosemary lives with her children, Xavier and Kayla and their dog Twix. She is also a member of the urban gospel group, Shekina N' Glory. In her free time, Rosemary enjoys spending time with her family, writing, lunch dates with friends, long walks and creating various forms of art.

ACKNOWLEDGMENTS

I would like to thank my church family at Redeeming Love Outreach Ministries and the vast body of believers of Jesus Christ that prayed and expressed an agape love towards my family. You were beams of radiant light in our darkest hour. Your labor of love will never be forgotten. To my pastor, Pastor Emma White, I thank you for laboring with me in faith and love through the entire journey. You taught me what faith looks like and how to walk by faith and not by sight. I am always grateful for your leadership and proud you are my pastor!

To Robert, thank you for the gift of our precious children.

Toya Poplar, thank you for supporting me throughout the entire process of writing my first book through my time of grief and in the midst of a pandemic. I am also grateful for all the photographs you've captured of my family over the years. The have become a priceless monument in my home.

Thanks to my family: My mom Linda and my little brother Lorenzo who always love and support me; Boniechia and Knegleshia, thank you for always being there for me, especially when I needed a listening ear to hear the pains and joys of my heart.

Rica, Katie, Mary Alice, and JoAnne, thank you for organizing Team Qe'Vonte and showing up for us through cooked meals, rides to doctor appointments, and even the surprise mini house makeover! Most of all, I'm grateful for how you loved my children. Your labor of love will never be forgotten.

CONTACT AND FOLLOW ROSEMARY SHERROD AT:

Email: believinginthedark@gmail.com and rosemary@believinginthedark.com

Website: www.believinginthedark.com

Facebook: @BelievingInTheDark

Instagram: @believinginthedark

THIS BOOK IS AVAILABLE THROUGH AMAZON AND OTHER ONLINE RETAILERS.

ENDNOTES

1. Statistics adapted from the American Cancer Society website.
    Additional source was: Seigel R, et al.: Cancer Statistics 2021.
    CA: A Cancer Journal for Clinicians. 2021 Jan; 71(1):7-33.
    doi/full/10.3322/caac.21654 (sources accessed January 2021).

CPSIA information can be obtained
at www.ICGtesting.com
Printed in the USA
LVHW081256040122
707822LV00019B/170